DAWN
OVER
SARATOGA:
The Turning Point of the Revolutionary War

by Fred J. Cook

Doubleday & Company, Inc., Garden City, New York

ISBN: 0-385-04105-5 TRADE
      0-385-04150-0 PREBOUND
Library of Congress Catalog Card Number 72–92199
Copyright © 1973 by Fred J. Cook
All Rights Reserved
Printed in the United States of America
First Edition

CHAPTER ONE

The Cast

THEY WERE the most colorful cast of characters ever to contend on one battlefield in American history, and the drama they played out resulted in the birth of a nation.

The year was 1777. The Revolutionary War, begun two years earlier at Lexington and Concord, had been a series of almost unrelieved disasters for the patriot cause. The British, forced out of Boston, had seized the great port of New York, and an invasion fleet that would have dwarfed the famed Spanish Armada turned the harbor white with its sails and poured ashore thousands upon thousands of the best troops in Europe. This overwhelming army had chased George Washington's ragged Continentals all over the state of New Jersey at the end of 1776, and the patriot cause had been saved from utter collapse by a stroke of daring and genius. At Christmas time Washington had crossed the ice-choked Delaware, had surprised a celebrating enemy force at Trenton, and had rounded up a large bag of prisoners in a counterstroke that had stunned the overconfident enemy. Then he had taken his ragtag army into winter quarters in the northern New Jersey hills around Morristown, a vantage point from which he could watch the British in New York and ponder where the next mighty blow might fall.

Opportunity seemed to sit upon the British doorstep, waiting to be embraced. The strategy was so obvious that Washington himself could not imagine that the enemy would not see and seize it. The situation was this:

The British had turned back a puny and foolhardy American attempt to invade Canada in the early stages of the war. Now they had a mighty army poised there. In New York City they had the supremely powerful army that had belabored Washington with defeat after defeat. Between these two separated forces lay an inviting watery avenue, stretching all the way from New York to the Canadian border. The chain ran up the Hudson River from New York and threaded into Lake George and Lake Champlain; it was broken only by short stretches of trackless wilderness. It was a highway ideal for the transportation of invading armies and their supplies; it was an invitation to victory.

A strike from Canada down Lake Champlain, Lake George, and the Hudson; a strike up the Hudson by that huge British army in New York; a linkup at Albany—and the rebellious thirteen colonies would be divided. New England, the hotbed of the Revolution, would be separated from all the colonies to the south and could be chewed up piecemeal, at British leisure.

Disaster stared the Americans in the face, but the result, incredibly, was to be their greatest victory—the Battle of Saratoga, which historians were to rate as among the most decisive in the history of the world, the battle that turned around the whole floundering course of the Revolution. How could it ever have happened? The explanation lies in the bewildering cast of characters and the way, with both their strengths and their weaknesses, they acted upon one another. It was a drama in which timidity and caution laid a trap for gambling foolhardiness; a drama in which injured pride and pique placed the right general on the right field at the right time; a drama in which a man with the heart of a traitor became one of the heroes of the battlefield; a drama in which a half-wit all by himself routed an army. By every standard it was a drama that should never have happened —except that it did.

The principal figure on the British side was Lieutenant General John (Gentleman Johnny) Burgoyne, commander of the invading army from Canada. Tall and handsome, with large brilliant eyes and a strong, jutting, stubborn jaw, he had been a cavalry officer noted for his dash and daring on European battlefields; a playwright whose works had been performed successfully on the London stage; a reckless gambler in the London clubs, a man who at one point had almost wrecked his career because he bet not wisely and too much. Gentleman Johnny had many qualities rarely found among the generals of his time (after all, how many were familiar with Greek and Latin or capable of writing successful musical comedies?), but he had in abundance, too, the weaknesses of his class. He set out on his wilderness campaign accompanied by an obliging mistress he had picked up in Canada and with some thirty carts—despite the fact that such carts were in critically short supply—devoted to carrying her fripperies and his wines, wardrobe, and items of personal comfort.

Burgoyne's counterpart in command in New York was General Sir William Howe, tall, dark-complexioned, with a rather thick nose and snapping black eyes. Fearless on the battlefield, he was a dandy in his dress and a lover of fun and frivolity, a man who could be turned from delivering the final, crushing stroke on the battlefield by the sight of a pretty face and a well-turned ankle. Howe was a second cousin to King George III through the happy circumstance that his father had had the wit to marry an illegitimate daughter of King George I. A Member of Parliament, he was a Whig and believed, like other members of the party, that the war against the American colonies was wrong. But, given the job of fighting it, he fought well up to a point—but always stopped short of final success. He commanded with a kind of royal negligence, not bothering to read many of the letters and proclamations that his staff presented to him to sign. He devoted more time and attention to the charms of Mrs. Joshua Loring, wife of his brutal but complaisant Commissary of Prisoners, than he did to the grubby business of the battlefield. He was, to sum up, a man who liked his wine and his mistress and the gay life of his headquarters so much that he could rarely put his mind to grand strategy but was apt to go off, as he did in 1777, in any wayward direction in which he might be prodded.

The commanding general on the American side was Major General Horatio Gates, whose character was reflected in the nickname his men gave him—"Granny." A former professional soldier in the British Army, he was fifty at the time of Saratoga, but he looked and seemed much older. He was stooped, ruddy-cheeked; he had thinning gray hair and wore spectacles that seemed to be always precariously perched near the tip of his long nose. He has been called, with considerable justice, "an intriguer and a humbug." He was cautious and timid; he was inclined to oppose any move that might bring on a battle; he always seemed more prepared for defeat than for victory. Yet at Saratoga he had one great virtue—a canny insight into Burgoyne's character. He knew that Burgoyne was a reckless gambler, and he preferred to sit behind his entrenchments, doing nothing, forcing Burgoyne to gamble, and hoping that the wilderness stretching behind Burgoyne to Canada and the approach of the harsh northern winter would combine to finish off his enemy for him. Though the strategy was born of the ineptitude of its author, it was not in the circumstances such a bad strategy.

Gates's hand was forced, the battle was forced, by the fiery and tempestuous man who was to become the most famous traitor in American history—Major General Benedict Arnold. Short but powerfully built, Arnold had black hair, a dark complexion, and light blue eyes. From boyhood on, he had been the kind of man who would do anything, take any risk, just to attract attention to himself. He was a man filled with a vast sense of his own importance, one who liked to live in extravagant style far beyond his means, one whose ego was so huge that he would explode in fury at the least slight to his talents or, as he was forever calling it, his "sacred honor." At the time of Saratoga, he had indeed been slighted by the bumbling politicians in

Congress who had rewarded incompetents with higher rank on the ladder of command, and so he was seething with the kind of inner rage that, combined with other pressures, ulti-mately would lead him to betray his country. A flawed man with self-destroying weaknesses, Arnold had one supreme vir-tue: he was a tremendous fighter. On the battlefield, he dashed into flying bullets like a man who both courted death and defied it: in that element, he was a heroic figure who seemed to bear a charmed life and who could inspire men to follow him any-where.

Arnold's fighting counterpart—between the two of them, they would prod and drag the unwarlike Gates to battle—was Colonel Daniel Morgan, leader of the Virginia and Pennsylvania riflemen, veterans of the frontier Indian wars and the deadliest shots on the field at Saratoga. Dan Morgan was six feet tall, with massive shoulders and powerful arms. He hated the British with a purple passion as the result of a brutal punishment inflicted upon him by the British military in the French and Indian War. Then a teamster, he had been court-martialed for striking an officer; he had been trussed up and given a savage beating of several hundred lashes on his bare back—a punishment that would have killed a lesser man and that inflicted scars Morgan was to bear the rest of his life. A wily and resourceful frontier fighter, Morgan got his revenge at Saratoga, maneuvering his riflemen with his turkey-gobbler call, directing his sharpshooters in de-livering a withering fire that took a special toll of British officers.

Another famous Indian fighter, testy and cantankerous and unmanageable, a staunch patriot without the personal flaws that were to ruin Arnold, was Brigadier General John Stark of New Hampshire; and he, too, because he wouldn't take orders from anyone else, was to be at just the right spot at the right time, masterminding a battle that would lop off one of Burgoyne's invading arms. In his late forties, Stark had an enviable military reputation. He had marched with Roger's Rangers, the band of frontier scouts who had turned Indian tactics upon the French and Indians in the French and Indian War; he had fought

brilliantly at Bunker Hill; he had taken part in the ill-fated
invasion of Canada. But, like Arnold, he had been passed over
for promotion in the jealous political in-fighting in Congress;
nursing his wounded feelings, he had thrown up his commission
and returned to New Hampshire, vowing he would never again
serve in the Continental Army or accept orders from its commanders—nor did he. And so there he was, at home in the
New Hampshire hills, a fiercely bitter man, when the call came
for him to lead native militia forces at the Battle of Bennington
in Vermont, and he led so well that he wiped out a strong detachment of Burgoyne's army, inflicting a defeat that was to be
the beginning of the end.

There were others who played their roles, a host of minor
actors as individual and unique in their ways as the principals.
There was a long-tressed Tory girl named Jane McCrea, who
was engaged to an officer in Burgoyne's army—but who was
scalped by Burgoyne's uncontrollable, rampaging Indians. Her
fiancé recognized her distinctive long tresses when an Indian
named Wyandot Panther flaunted her scalp in camp, and Burgoyne suffered a propaganda defeat from which he never recovered. The lesson seemed plain: even a Tory girl was not safe
from the savages employed by her own side. Jane McCrea
became more beautiful and more tragic with each retelling of
her horrible fate, creating a legend that swept New England
and brought the aroused American militiamen buzzing like so
many hornets about Burgoyne's ears.

Among the host of other characters was the most unusual
rifleman of the Revolution—Timothy Murphy, a product of the
northern New Jersey and Pennsylvania frontiers; a scout who
had become the terror of the Indians in the Mohawk and
Schoharie valleys; a man noted for his unique weapon, a
double-barreled long rifle, and for the deadly marksman's eye
which led him to brag he had never missed a shot. In the final
phase of the Battle of Saratoga, it was Timothy Murphy who
was to fire probably the most important single shot of the war,
killing the inspiring British General Simon Fraser as he was

rallying his troops and, with this shot, spreading panic in British ranks.

All of these—and, of course, that half-wit who put an army to flight. But of him, more later.

CHAPTER TWO

Valcour Island

THE AMERICANS survived to win at Saratoga in 1777 only because that fey fighting man, Benedict Arnold, then a brigadier general, waged one of the most hopeless battles ever fought against overwhelming odds—and so delayed the British invasion from the north by a full year.

In late spring of 1776 the ragged handful of Americans who had invaded Canada began to straggle back down the chain of lakes. Though reinforcements had been sent north, the new soldiers and the old were ravaged by smallpox and other diseases. More a rabble than an army, they collapsed at the end of June around the ruins of Crown Point, a dilapidated fort on lower Lake Champlain, and around Fort Ticonderoga, ten miles to the south—a stronghold billed as the "Gibraltar of the North" that commanded the narrow, strategic channel linking Champlain with Lake George.

The condition of the troops was pitiable. John Adams, the great Massachusetts patriot, wrote: "Our Army at Crown Point is an object of wretchedness to fill a humane mind with horrour (*sic*); disgraced, defeated, discontented, diseased, naked, undisciplined, eaten up with vermin; no clothes, beds, blankets, no medicines; no victuals, but salt pork and flour."

Three thousand had been stricken with disease; they died by the hundreds and were flung into open burial pits. Colonel John Trumbull wrote to his father, the governor of Connecticut: "I can truly say that I did not look into a tent that did not contain a dead or dying man." Five thousand men had been lost in the Canadian adventure; some 5000 remained, mere specters, walking skeletons, barely able to drag themselves around, unable to fight.

In Canada the British were massing in new might. Sir Guy Carleton commanded there, with ambitious Gentleman Johnny Burgoyne as his second; and, once the ice had broken in the St. Lawrence River, the British fleet had poured into Canada such a spate of reinforcements that Carleton now commanded an army of 13,000 veteran soldiers, plus Indians and local militia. This land force was backed up by powerful British warships in the St. Lawrence, a fleet able to furnish Carleton with heavy cannon, abundant naval stores, and hundreds of skilled officers and sailors to handle his ships in the advance down the lakes.

It seemed like a contest between David and Goliath, only this American David was so ill and so weak he seemed to be tottering on the brink of his own grave, and he was further handicapped by chaotic leadership. It was not certain who commanded whom.

All of the rivalries, all of the clashes of personalities that were to mark so dramatically the campaign of 1777 had their preview in the crisis of 1776. The commander of the Northern Department at the time of the invasion of Canada had been Major General Philip Schuyler. Schuyler was a patrician, the owner of estates covering thousands of acres in upper New York, an aristocratic rebel like his good friend, George Washington.

As tall as Washington, Schuyler was lanky but powerfully built, with aquiline features, brown eyes, and reddish brown hair. He had the imposing, commanding presence of a true general, but he was no fighting field commander. He was hampered by poor health, suffering attacks of rheumatic gout, an illness that plagued him all his life, and so he was rarely in the field; his troops seldom saw him.

Schuyler was, however, an excellent organizer and a man who possessed considerable strategic vision. During the Canadian campaign, he had remained behind at headquarters in Albany, trying to raise reinforcements and keep supplies flowing to the invading army. The actual fighting had been left to Benedict Arnold and Major General Richard Montgomery, a gallant field commander who was killed in the desperate attempt to storm Quebec. Later, during the long retreat, Major General John Sullivan had been in command of the troops in the field.

Though the Canadian invasion had been foredoomed to disaster by lack of manpower and equipment, the retreat down the lakes shook up the jittery politicians in the Continental Congress, and they rushed to the north a savior in the person of Horatio Gates. Gates and Schuyler were contrasting types, symbols of forces that have clashed again and again in American history. Schuyler was the great landed proprietor, the gentlemanly aristocrat, aloof and distrustful of the rabble; Gates, the slovenly dressed, unassuming "Granny," who courted the favor of his soldiers and considered himself a man of the common people, a radical democrat. New Englanders, those hell-raisers of the Revolution, distrusted the courtly Schuyler, who reminded them too much of British officer-aristocrats whom they hated. On the other hand, they looked upon "Granny" Gates as one of their own, a common-man type of general whose devotion to the radical cause could not be doubted.

The appointment of Gates to the northern command at once created the question of who was to have the over-all northern command—Gates or Schuyler? Each had partisans in Congress, and the politicians in typical political fashion tried to straddle the issue and please everybody. Schuyler, they decreed, should retain command of all forces in New York State; Gates should command the army in Canada. The trouble was, of course, that there was no army in Canada. Gates considered that he had been appointed to command the army, period. Schuyler insisted he was still the boss. It was the kind of snafu that did not encourage friendly relations; and it was not settled until July 8 when Congress passed a resolution notifying Gates that its previous decision had not been intended "to vest him with a superior command to General Schuyler."

Before word of this decision could reach the isolated northern command, the generals themselves had reached a temporary settlement of their tangled affairs. Schuyler, Gates, Arnold, and Sullivan conferred on July 5 at Crown Point and, under Schuyler's guidance, came to a decision that was to become all-important in holding up the British and delaying their invasion at a time when the Americans were weakest. The decision was to build a navy to contest the British advance down Lake Champlain.

The Americans had the nucleus of a fleet in ships captured from the British the previous year. They had the schooners *Royal Savage* and *Liberty,* the sloop *Enterprise,* all taken from the British, and the schooner *Revenge,* built at Ticonderoga. This was a small force with pop-gun armaments to use in battle against British vessels having at their disposal the enormous resources of the fleet in the St. Lawrence. It was obvious to Schuyler that more ships would have to be built—and built swiftly.

The high-command conference at Crown Point broke up with the leaders assigned to individual tasks and, for the moment, co-operating well. Schuyler went back to Albany and devoted himself to the business of rounding up shipbuilders and supplies; Gates remained in command of the forces in the field, based on Ticonderoga; and Arnold took charge of the fleet on Lake Champlain.

This last selection was a natural one. Arnold, like so many of the multiskilled men of the Revolution, was an accomplished sailor as well as a general. Beginning as a Connecticut merchant, he had acquired his own small trading ships and had sailed them to the West Indies. His knowledge of ship handling made him, as Gates put it, "perfectly skilled in naval affairs."

Typically, Arnold threw himself into his new role as fleet commander with all of the furious, driving energy for which he was so remarkable. Soldiers were set to felling trees; creaky sawmills were repaired and put to work carving up green lumber;

keels were laid, vessels built. Some 200 ship's carpenters, promised what in those times was the incredible sum of five dollars
a day in "hard money," were lured from the shipyards of
Massachusetts, Connecticut, Rhode Island—and some from
even as far away as Philadelphia—and were sent north by
Schuyler, together with all the nautical supplies he could round
up.

The jerry-built fleet was put together at Skenesborough (now
Whitehall), a hamlet on Wood Creek on the east side of Lake
Champlain—a tiny wilderness settlement that, ironically, was
to play a pivotal role in Burgoyne's campaign the following
year. Here, with Arnold rushing furiously all around the countryside, rounding up workers, badgering superiors for supplies,
Brigadier General David Waterbury, of Connecticut, took direct
charge of the shipbuilding effort.

Two types of vessels were constructed: row galleys and gondolas. The galleys were larger. They were round-bottomed, about
eighty feet long and eighteen feet in beam. They had two masts
equipped with lateen sails like those used by Barbary corsairs in
the Mediterranean—a decidedly unusual rig, which was adopted
because it was thought it would be easier for landlubbers to
handle. In calm weather, the galleys were rowed by thirty-six
sweeps. Each was to carry a crew of eighty men and have from
ten to twelve guns, two in the bow, the rest in broadside.

The gondolas were smaller, little more than glorified row-
boats. They were forty-five feet long, carried forty-five men
each, and each had a mast rigged with two square sails. They
were slower and more cumbersome than the galleys; they were
able to sail only before the wind; and they carried just three
guns, one that fired a twelve-pound ball and two nine-pounders.

This shipbuilding effort by the Americans at the south end of
the lake compelled Carleton to pause at the north end and put
together a fleet of his own. Because the British resources were
so much larger, it was a one-sided contest. Still, it had one
advantage for the Americans: it delayed the British; it took time.
In the fleet that Carleton finally assembled, two of the warships
alone were more than a match for the entire American flotilla.

One was the three-masted ship *Inflexible,* which Carleton had taken apart in the St. Lawrence, hauled overland by sections, and put together again at the head of the lake. The other was a huge, raftlike affair named the *Thunderer,* a kind of floating fortress carrying 300 men and armed with six huge twenty-four-pounders, six twelve-pounders, and two heavy howitzers.

Ever the impatient man of action, Arnold took to the lake and sailed north even before his fleet was completed. Vessel by vessel, as they were hastily outfitted, they left the shipyards and sailed north to try to catch up with him. They were lacking in almost everything. Their crews were as green as the green lumber from which they had been constructed. Right up to the eve of battle, Arnold kept writing Gates, pleading for better sailors and more supplies. "Great part of those who shipped for seamen know very little of the matter," he wrote in one letter. In another: "We have a wretched, motley crew in the fleet, the marines the refuse of every regiment, and the seamen few of them ever wet with salt water." He needed gunners, he wrote, because few of his men knew anything about sighting and handling a cannon. He needed clothing for his men, for the fall nights were getting cold on Lake Champlain. He got nothing —neither the clothes nor the seamen nor the gunners.

Instead, he got words of caution from Gates. Risk nothing. Expose neither himself nor his vessels. Annoy the enemy if he could, but keep clear of him. To Arnold such orders were ridiculous. Nobody would ever call him "Granny." Warships, in Arnold's view, had been built to fight.

Knowing that he was outgunned by the British, he selected the proposed site of battle with care. The spot he chose was Valcour Island, about two thirds of the way up Lake Champlain. The island was close to the western, or New York, shore. It was hilly and heavily wooded, and the channel down the lake, narrower here, ran past the island on its eastern side. Arnold decided that it was an ideal spot to set a trap.

The British could come down the lake only with a good north breeze behind them. Arnold's tiny fleet, hidden from view behind the island, was anchored in a half-moon formation, facing south, across the half-mile gap of water between the island and the lake's western shore. If everything worked right, the British would sweep past the eastern edge of the island before they discovered Arnold's fleet. Then, not being able to leave this force in their rear, they would have to come about and try to beat back to the attack in the teeth of the north wind—a maneuver that, Arnold calculated, might throw their ships into disarray and make them unable to bring all their fire power to bear on him at once.

Carleton sailed from St. Johns at the northern end of the lake on October 4. His fleet was led by the *Inflexible* and the *Thunderer*. With them were the schooners *Maria* and *Carleton*, the gondola *Loyal Convert*, twenty gunboats, and four long-boats with fieldpieces in their bows. The British squadron, commanded by Captain Thomas Pringle, of the Royal Navy, advanced cautiously. Pringle tried to scout out the position of the American vessels on the lake, but he failed to get the information that might have helped him. And so, on October 11, 1776, he did just what Arnold had hoped he would do—he rounded Cumberland Head with a north wind behind him, sailed past the eastern side of Valcour Island, and did not discover Arnold's hidden fleet until he had passed well to the south.

The British ships came about in disorder and tried to beat back against the now-hostile north wind. This blunder by Pringle, however, was now matched by one by Arnold himself. Having planned a defensive battle, Arnold could not resist the urge to attack when he saw the British ships floundering about. He ordered the *Royal Savage* and four galleys to strike at the enemy. He led the sortie himself in the galley *Congress*. Once out in the lake, he realized even more fully than he had before the overwhelming odds he faced—a fleet that could throw some 500 pounds of deadly metal in one broadside against the Americans' 265. Quickly Arnold changed his mind and ordered the *Royal Savage* and galleys to return to their original line. The galleys got back into formation, but the *Royal Savage* was so badly handled that she ran aground on Valcour Island, all but helpless before the guns of the British fleet and subjected to musketry fire from Canadians and Indians that the British landed on the island.

Battle was now joined, and the cleverness of Arnold's strategy quickly became apparent. The most powerful British warships were caught out in the lake, unable to beat back against the wind. The huge *Thunderer* never did get a chance to thunder in battle. The *Inflexible, Maria,* and *Loyal Convert* were all trapped in the battle with the wind instead of the battle with the Americans. Only the *Carleton* and seventeen British gunboats managed to get in close and open fire from a distance of about 350 yards.

"A tremendous cannonade was opened on both sides," Baron Friedrich von Riedesel, commander of Carleton's German troops, later wrote.

The firing began about noon and lasted until nearly nightfall. The stranded *Royal Savage* became a special target. Her crew stuck by her as long as they could, working what guns would bear. But the British concentrated their fire on the helpless ship; she was swept by musketry shots from Valcour Island; and she was finally abandoned. A boat crew from the *Thunderer* took possession and turned the schooner's guns on the Americans. This drew such hot counterfire that the *Thunderer*'s men were forced to flee. Finally, another boat crew from the *Maria* boarded the *Royal Savage* and set her afire, and she blew up.

In the meantime, the main battle raged between the *Carleton* and the British gunboats on one side and Arnold's anchored galleys and gondolas on the other. The British gunboats did considerable damage, and they sat so low in the water they made difficult targets for Arnold's inexperienced gunners to hit. The *Carleton* was a different matter.

This British schooner got in too close to the American line for her own good. She anchored almost opposite Arnold's *Congress* and blazed away. The guns of almost the entire American flotilla were trained in turn upon this lone, inviting target. The *Carleton* was hulled again and again. Her captain was knocked senseless; another officer lost an arm. Command finally devolved upon Edward Pellew, then only a midshipman but later to become famous as a British admiral. Pellew fought for his vessel stubbornly until the cable that held her in position was shot away. The *Carleton* then swung bow on to the American fleet and hung there. Since she had no bow guns, she could not fire a shot, and the American fire raked her from stem to stern. Captain Pringle on the *Maria* out in the lake signaled to Pellew to withdraw, but the *Carleton*'s sails were so riddled there was not a rag left to catch the wind.

In this desperate situation, young Pellew ran out on the bowsprit and tried to set a jib while musket balls whizzed all around him. The piece of canvas he managed to hoist would not draw, but he and the *Carleton* were rescued finally when two boats from the British fleet rowed in, got a towline aboard, and towed the schooner away. She had two feet of water in her hold, and half her crew were dead or wounded.

Now, near the end of the long afternoon, the *Inflexible* finally worked her way up against the wind and swung around into position opposite the American line. Her long twelve-pounders fired again and again, five crashing broadsides delivered at point-blank range, sweeping the American line. The hail of the heavier cannon balls silenced the American guns. Night was now coming on, and the *Inflexible,* her job done, drew back, followed by the British gunboats. They anchored in a line across the southern end of the passage between Valcour Island and the western shore. There they waited for morning when, they expected, they could finish off the Americans at their ease.

As the firing died away, Arnold took stock. His ships had battered the *Carleton* and sunk three British gunboats, but his little fleet was in pitiable shape. His own *Congress* had two cannon balls lodged in her mainmast; she had been hulled twelve times and had two holes in her side between wind and water. The galley *Washington* had a shot in her mainmast and had been severely punished. The hull of the galley *Philadelphia* had been so riddled that she sank an hour after the battle ended. Same sixty Americans had been killed or wounded; three quarters of their ammunition had been exhausted; their ships' sails had been torn to tatters and their rigging was in tangled ruins. Surrender seemed inevitable, but surrender was a word that did not exist in Benedict Arnold's vocabulary.

The night was dark, and a heavy fog came up, shrouding the two fleets. Under its cover, hoisting a few patched rags of sails, Arnold's vessels crept silently away, slipping past the British fleet. When day dawned, the astonished British stared out on empty water. Their prey had fled.

Furious, Carleton and Pringle took up the pursuit. So angry were they that they forgot all about the soldiers they had put ashore; and when they remembered them, they had to lose precious time coming about and retracing their course to pick up the stranded men. Taking advantage of the delay, the American ships fled south down the lake.

The *Revenge* and *Enterprise* and the galley *Trumbull,* accompanied by some of the gondolas, were in fairly good shape and soon outdistanced the rest. Wallowing behind were the badly damaged galleys *Congress* and *Washington* and the gondolas *Providence, New York,* and *Jersey.* After making only eight miles, Arnold put in at Schuyler Island and examined his ships. The *New York* and *Providence* were found to be in such bad shape that their equipment was transferred to the other vessels and they were sunk. The *Jersey* ran aground and had so much water in her that she could not be moved—and so was abandoned.

This left just the *Congress* and the *Washington* to continue the flight. The wind now shifted to the south and blew hard in their faces. Arnold kept his men rowing for sixteen straight hours, but they gained only six miles. Four of the gondolas that had gone on ahead of them, buffeted by the head wind, fell back and joined them. This was the tiny force on which the British pounced when they came charging down the lake as the wind shifted again to the north.

The *Inflexible,* the patched-up *Carleton,* and the *Maria* led the attack. They caught up with the *Washington* first, and General Waterbury, who had commanded her throughout the battle, struck his colors. This left only the *Congress* and the four gondolas.

Any one of the British ships should have been more than a match for the *Congress,* but Arnold fought all three in a running battle that lasted two and a half hours. Broadside to broadside he pounded one of his foes while the two others smashed the *Congress'* stern to splinters. Still Arnold would not surrender.

He signaled to the four gondolas to put out sweeps, rowing for the eastern shore against a head wind that held back the British sailing ships. Then, painfully, still firing whatever guns would work, he rowed the waterlogged *Congress* after them into the shelter of Buttonmould Bay. There he beached his wrecks and set them afire, their flags still flying. He ranged his men up on the shore, the 200 survivors, and waited until the ships blew up. Then he led his ragged band overland to Crown Point.

Arnold had been utterly defeated. He had lost some eighty men killed and wounded, another 110 taken prisoners; he had lost eleven of the sixteen ships with which he had begun the battle. Carleton had turned the lake into a British duck pond. He had won a victory—but, in winning, had been defeated.

Arnold had cost Carleton time he did not have to lose, first in the shipbuilding race, then in the maneuvering on the lake, finally in the long, running battle. It was now mid-October; the British had been themselves badly knocked about; and the harsh northern winter was almost upon them. Carleton decided it was too late to attack Fort Ticonderoga, and so he withdrew up the lake to Canada.

The desperate, hopeless Battle of Valcour Island had won the Americans a year—a vital year that was to make possible the greatest victory of the war. Captain Alfred Thayer Mahan, the great expert on naval strategy, would later write that the American victory at Saratoga in 1777 "was due to the invaluable year of delay secured to them in 1776 by their little navy on Lake Champlain, created by the indomitable energy, and handled by the indomitable courage of the traitor, Benedict Arnold."

The Battle of Valcour Island had one other lasting effect, this one involving personal relationships between American generals. "Granny" Gates would never have fought such a battle. To his cautious mind, only a madman would have acted and fought

as Arnold had; and from this point on, it seemed, he distrusted
Arnold, viewing him as a blood-crazed fighter who must be kept
on a tight leash—an attitude that was to bring the two into
head-on collision in the whirlwind storms of Saratoga a year
later.

CHAPTER THREE

Gentleman Johnny's Plans

GENTLEMAN JOHNNY BURGOYNE's military career followed a pattern. He fought the American rebels during the good summer campaigning months; but once the cold northern winter approached, he took the first ship back to England, there to enjoy the pleasures of London until it was time to fight again. And it was notable that each time he returned to America, he came back in a higher position than the one he had held when he left.

In the early stages of the war, he had been third in command in Boston. He made the winter pilgrimage to England and returned the next spring as second in command to Carleton. As soon as the campaign of 1776 ended, it was back to London again for Gentleman Johnny—and another leap, this time right over Carleton's head.

This command-grabbing feat was made possible because Gentleman Johnny had a gambler's eye for the main chance—and contacts in circles where contacts counted. He had been this way all his life. As a young student at Westminster School, he had cultivated the friendship of Lord Strange, heir to the eleventh Earl of Derby. Through Lord Strange, he had become acquainted with the other members of the family; and before anyone realized what was happening, Gentleman Johnny had made off with a young and pretty daughter of the earl, the Lady Charlotte Stanley. The following year, 1744, he joined the 1st Royal Dragoons.

The elopement and marriage outraged the Earl of Derby so much that he banished the brash young couple from his presence. Gentleman Johnny, heavily in debt from his reckless gambling in the London gaming houses, had to sell his commission (this was an age in which rank was bought and sold) to get his head above water. There followed a few tough years, but the event seemed to say that no one could resist the charm of Gentleman Johnny for long. The Derby family ended by forgiving all, becoming his sponsors, and buying him a commission as a captain in the 11th Dragoons. Gentleman Johnny was on his way.

He whipped his command into such shape that it became known as one of the crack outfits in the British Army. King George III, soon after he ascended the throne, was so impressed with the regiment's color and dash that he never tired of inspecting it and finally conferred upon it the title of the Queen's Light Dragoons. Gentleman Johnny thus had a lot of pull, both through the powerful Derby family and with the King himself, when he returned to England in late 1776 with a plan that he felt sure would end the war—and, by no means incidentally, make him famous.

Burgoyne's idea was not entirely new. It was really only a more imaginative elaboration of the strategy on which Carleton had campaigned in 1776. Basically, it was the same old plan of splitting the American colonies by an invasion down the water route from Canada to New York, but Burgoyne added important embellishments to the slapdash strategy of the past.

What he proposed was an overwhelming three-pronged attack. The major drive, whose commander would of course reap the greatest glory—and who would of course be Gentleman Johnny himself—would be launched from Canada. This southward thrust would be co-ordinated with an attack up the Hudson by the all-powerful army of Sir William Howe in New York. The patriot forces, caught between these pincers, would be further sliced up and distracted by a third force, composed largely of Tories and Indians, that would invade western New York from a base at Oswego on Lake Ontario. After seizing the rebels' weak frontier forts, this third arm of the invasion forces would slash down the Mohawk Valley and link up with Burgoyne and Howe at Albany. The American armies would be splintered and crushed, the rebellion ended in one smashing campaign. This was the glorious vision.

On paper, the strategy looked foolproof, and perhaps it would have been had not so many fools meddled with it. It should have been obvious from the outset that the victory Burgoyne envisioned depended to a great degree upon co-operation by Howe. If Howe did not come charging up the Hudson, Burgoyne's army would be left alone to fight the Americans and wrestle with the hardships of the wilderness. In describing his plan, Burgoyne in places seemed to realize this and yet, in other sections, he obviously toyed with the fascinating notion of being able to complete the job all by himself—and, of course, reap all the glory. Typical was this passage in his outline:

"These ideas are formed upon the supposition that it be the sole purpose of the army in Canada to effect a junction with General Howe; *or,* after co-operating so far as to get possession of Albany and open the communication to New-York, to remain upon the Hudson's-River, and *thereby enable that general to act with his whole force to the southward . . .*" (Emphasis added)

That one little word "or" was to be fatal. There was no room for "or" in Burgoyne's plan if it were to succeed; victory depended upon a positive, co-ordinated strategy.

King George III, in endorsing the scheme, did not catch the queasiness and imprecision implicit in Burgoyne's "or." He evidently suffered under the misconception that his top generals were capable and that the Colonial Department under Lord George Germain was not run by an idiot. He therefore approved what he thought was Burgoyne's plan, and in a memorandum in his own handwriting noted that "the force from Canada *must* join him [Howe] at Albany." (Emphasis added)

The King's "must" made no impression, however, upon the

incredible bungler who had been put in charge of the American war. Lord George Germain had been sacked as a British field officer for failing to obey orders; but, in the nature of things, coming from a noble family with a lot of political clout, he had lived down this disgrace and had wound up as the overlord of generals and armies.

Had he been less of a blunderer it would have been obvious to him that any uncertainty about the campaigns of the widely separated British armies invited disaster. One account of the times asserts that subordinates in the Colonial Department did point out to Germain that Howe had not been notified in positive terms of what was expected of him. The reminder, however, came at an inopportune moment. Lord George had an engagement and was impatient. "So," said he, "my poor horses must stand in the street all the time [while a message was being prepared for Howe], and I shan't be to my time anywhere." Not a man to keep his horses waiting, Germain rushed off, and Howe never did get the kind of clear, explicit instructions he should have had.

Germain's horses, however, cannot bear all the blame. Germain himself soon had very good cause to know that his generals, instead of striking together, were planning to ride off in all directions like headless horsemen. Germain came to know this because Howe told him.

That pleasure-loving general, whiling away the winter of 1776–77 in New York at routs and balls and capers with the beauteous Mrs. Loring, had conceived an idea at complete odds with Burgoyne's. Ignoring the obvious advantages of a unified northern campaign, he decided to go off in exactly the opposite direction, striking to the *southward* at the rebel capital of Philadelphia.

Whatever possessed Howe? This remains a considerable mystery. The most logical explanation seems to be that the genial general imagined that, once he had captured the rebels' capital, the rebels would see the futility of fighting and would lay down their arms. There is some evidence also that he was encouraged to think "south" instead of "north" by one of the most unstable and intriguing rogues in the Continental Army.

This was none other than Major General Charles Lee. A one-time British soldier and later a soldier-of-fortune during a period when Britain stopped having wars on the European Continent, Lee had become infuriated, as had Horatio Gates, to find himself shelved on half pay, with promotion to higher rank barred to him because he lacked noble connections and influence. In his resentment, he became a fiery democrat, and the American patriots became much enamored of him.

When the Continental Army was formed, Lee became second in command to Washington. This galled him. He always thought he should have been first. Nevertheless, he performed well until the disastrous campaign of 1776. Then, as Washington's army was chased all over New Jersey, Lee found himself to the north of New York, on the east side of the Hudson in Westchester County, with a powerful wing of the army and what amounted to a separate command. This he relished. Washington wrote letter after letter, urging Lee to join him; but Lee, when he finally crossed the Hudson, dallied in northern New Jersey, flatly disobeying his commander in chief's orders.

Then, on the night of December 12, 1776, he committed an unpardonable blunder. Leaving his troops, he sought more comfortable quarters for himself in a tavern at Basking Ridge, some three miles from his camp. He had only a small guard with him. Early the next morning he had just finished breakfast and was writing a short letter to his kindred spirit in spite and envy, Horatio Gates. One line read: "Entre nous, a certain great man [Washington, of course] is damnably deficient." Lee had barely finished his letter when a company of British dragoons charged up the lane, routed his small guard, and captured the general as he sat there in his robe and carpet slippers. Not giving him time to dress, the dragoons flung him on his horse, slippers and all, and carried him off to the British camp. There, to celebrate their triumph, they proceeded to get his poor horse drunk.

In such fashion, one of the most devious schemers in the

Continental Army landed in the lap of Sir William Howe. Howe treated Lee well, gave him spacious quarters, let him have fellow officers whom he had known in the British Army in to dine—and, eventually, it seems, discussed the problems and strategy of the war with him. Neither man left any record of these conversations, but there does exist a curious document, a letter from Lee to Howe that smells of treason. The letter probably put in formal shape ideas that had been discussed much earlier. In it Lee outlined a plan by which, he promised, the British could put down the rebellion in two months, and it seems significant that the strategy Lee advocated was in many important respects the strategy that Howe followed.

Lee's letter was dated March 29, 1777, and it held out to Howe the rosiest prospects for the success of a campaign in the South. Lee urged Howe to send troops up the "Patomac" to occupy Alexandria, Virginia, and to send the British fleet and supporting troops up "Chesepeak Bay" to seize "Anapolis." If Howe did this and then issued a proclamation pardoning all erring rebels, "I will answer for it with my life that all of the Inhabitants of that great tract southward of the Patapisco and lying betwixt the Patomac and Chesepeak Bay, and those on the Eastern Shore of Maryland will immediately lay down their arms."

Throughout the war, British commanders—Burgoyne himself was to be no exception—were constantly beguiled by the expectation that the entire countryside would rise to join them once they showed themselves in force. They just could not imagine (and in this they were not much different from American policy-makers in Vietnam nearly 200 years later) that a bunch of rustic colonial yokels would become so possessed with the fanaticism of freedom that they would fight on and on against imperial authority backed by overwhelming military might. Lee, for whatever purpose, dangled this enchanting prospect under Howe's long, thick nose; and Howe bought large chunks of the intriguer's plan.

He informed Germain that he was moving south against Philadelphia, and on March 3 Germain wrote him to go ahead.

It is obvious that the incompetent Germain could have had no conception of what he was doing. On the one hand, he had approved Burgoyne's complicated three-pronged invasion plan, a vital element of which called for a drive north by Howe; on the other, he sanctioned Howe's proposal to go off with his army in exactly the opposite direction, leaving Burgoyne to his own devices.

Burgoyne himself, if he had not learned of this switch in strategy before, certainly could have had no doubt about it after he arrived in Canada. Later, facing defeat at Saratoga, he would sit and wait and pray for succor from New York. But Howe, in a letter addressed to Carleton on April 2, 1777, had made it clear that he would be in no position to aid Burgoyne in any important way. By the time the Canadian invasion force reached Fort Ticonderoga, Howe wrote, "I shall probably be in Pennsylvania," and he added that "it will not be in my power to communicate with the officer commanding it so soon as I could wish; he must therefore pursue such measures as may from circumstances be judged most conducive to the advancement of his Majesty's service . . ." All Howe promised was a relatively minor diversion to attack American forts guarding the highland gorge on the lower Hudson.

The personal weaknesses, the incompetence, the outright stupidity of the men at the top were brewing an incomparable disaster for the British. At the time, hardly any competent officer in either the British or American camps could understand how so many brains in high position could have failed to see the obvious. Sir Henry Clinton, second in command to Howe, later wrote: "I owe it to truth to say there was not I believe a man in the Army except Lord Cornwallis and General Grant who did not reprobate the movement to the southward and see the necessity of cooperation with General Burgoyne." A captured British officer wrote after Saratoga that a major on Washington's staff told him that when Washington was informed of Howe's move to the South, "he did not believe it: he dreaded nothing so much as General Howe's Army going up the North [Hudson] River."

Blunderers all, the high and mighty were turning the promise of victory into the certainty of disaster. Charles Lee, dipping his pen in the venom of which only he was capable, summed up Sir William Howe, one of the chief culprits, in these words: "He shut his eyes, fought his battles, drunk his bottle, had his little whore, received his orders from North [Lord North, the British Prime Minister] and Germain, one more stupid than the other, shut his eyes and fought again."

As for Gentleman Johnny Burgoyne, he was so supremely confident that it did not matter to him at the moment where Howe went. Before he left London, he encountered Charles Fox in White's, a famous private club for the sporting gentry, and he bet the Whig orator, who opposed the war, fifty golden guineas that he would come back a hero, with the rebellion crushed. Even after he arrived in Canada, fully aware that Howe would not be on hand to help him, Gentleman Johnny had no qualms. He would conquer those pesky rebels all by himself; he would return to Britain the conquering hero, be made a peer of the realm—and collect those fifty golden guineas from Charles Fox.

CHAPTER FOUR

The Campaign Begins

IT HAD BEEN a mild winter in Canada. Snow melted early; ice in the St. Lawrence River broke up "with an astonishing noise" at the end of April. And along with the early spring came Gentleman Johnny Burgoyne, who disembarked at Quebec on May 6, two weeks ahead of schedule.

Burgoyne brought with him Germain's orders giving him command of the army in the field and reducing Sir Guy Carleton to the humble role of Canadian housekeeper. Germain, who hated Carleton, sent him a long and insulting letter, informing him of his changed status. The letter, in effect, accused Carleton of cowardliness for not having taken Fort Ticonderoga the previous year; it even blamed Carleton, incredible as it may seem, for the British debacle at far-off Trenton. Carleton had no choice but to resign, which he promptly did; but in the meantime, until he could be replaced, he labored as hard for Burgoyne as he would have for himself.

By Germain's orders, the British forces in Canada were divided in this fashion: Carleton was left with 3770 British and German troops to protect the home base; Burgoyne, with 7213 rank and file, plus Canadians and Tories, plus Indians, was to undertake the invasion down the lakes; Lieutenant Colonel Barry St. Leger with 675 men, plus a large contingent of Tories and Indians, would invade western New York and strike down the Mohawk Valley toward Albany.

The main army under Burgoyne was greatly encumbered. Having been in Boston at the time of the Battle of Breed's Hill (better, though inaccurately, known as Bunker Hill), Burgoyne had witnessed the carnage that sharpshooting colonial woodsmen could inflict when firing from the protection of entrenchments. This memory seems to have affected his thinking and his strategy. He determined to drag with him such a train of heavy artillery that, if he encountered rebels in any such entrenchments, he would be able to blast them out. His cannon ranged all the way from small field guns to huge twenty-four pounders; even in the latter stages of the campaign, he still had forty-two pieces in his field train—and nearly 240 horses were required just to drag these guns along.

As if this were not encumbrance enough, Burgoyne set out with an enormous amount of excess baggage. He had only some 500 carts, hastily put together from green lumber, to carry the provisions, powder, and supplies for his army. He reserved thirty of these scarce carts for his own and his mistress' paraphernalia; more were devoted to lugging along 1000 gallons of rum, to provide daily rations for an estimated thirty-day campaign; more still, to carrying some of the effects of the ragtag swarm of camp followers and children that trailed along with the army. A lot of these women were soldiers' drabs, but there were some 500 who were carried, as the saying was, "on the strength"—that is, they were soldiers' wives, and they were carried on the payroll returns and drew regular rations, in return for which they performed such chores as laundering and cooking.

All of this excess baggage, human and otherwise, could be carried comfortably enough as long as Burgoyne had the use of the British fleet on the lakes. The pinch would come when he had to set out overland through the short stretch of wilderness between Lake George and the Hudson. Burgoyne estimated that some 1400 horses would be needed then to transport his army in the style to which he had become accustomed, but at this point in his planning he confronted a difficulty: there weren't many horses in Canada. Just how many Burgoyne managed to get isn't clear, but records show that, by the time he reached the end of the lakes, he had only 637 and more than one third of these were needed just to haul his cannon.

In addition to all these handicaps, there was uncertainty from the outset about whether Burgoyne could count on any help from Howe. Carleton showed him Howe's letter of April 2, with its announcement of the Philadelphia campaign and its indication of only a minor diversion on the lower Hudson to aid Burgoyne; and Burgoyne seems to have wavered back and forth, at one moment wishing for aid from Howe, at the next almost hoping that Howe wouldn't come to share in the anticipated glory. Perhaps to clear himself in any eventuality, he twice wrote to Howe before he set out, emphasizing that his own orders were very "precise to force a junction" with Howe—a junction that obviously couldn't be accomplished if Howe were chasing off to Philadelphia.

The army assembled at St. Johns on June 13 with great bombast and pageantry. St. Johns was the Canadian stronghold on the Richelieu River that flowed southward into Lake Champlain. Here was anchored the British fleet that had been so victorious in the Battle of Valcour Island the year before. The mighty *Thunderer* was decked out with the royal standard of Great Britain—the red lion of Scotland, the harp of Ireland, and the fleur-de-lis of France, this as a tribute to the help anticipated from French-Canadian allies. When Burgoyne appeared, the guns of the *Thunderer,* the fort, and the rest of the fleet roared out in a thunderous salute whose echoes resounded over the wooded hillsides and across the quiet waters of river and lake, as if to warn the American rebels of their approaching doom.

The army was in fine fettle, its arms bright and well cared for. There were 3724 British regulars, 3016 crack German troops, an artillery detachment, a Canadian-Tory force—and the Indians. The traditional bright red British uniform with its long-tailed coat had undergone some surgery since new uni-

forms had not arrived and many of the old coats had to be
patched. The patches were obtained by clipping off the coattails,
reducing the coats to jackets. In similar fashion, the customary
high cocked hats that the soldiers wore had been cropped to
caps, with the different regiments designated by tufts of dyed
hair sewn into the crowns. The acquisition of these tufts had
provoked some disagreements with the inhabitants of the
countryside. The soldiers had discovered that the white hair
from cows' tails best absorbed the brightly colored dyes, and
many Canadians became incensed at finding themselves the own-
ers of suddenly tailless cows.

Burgoyne was disappointed at the size of the Canadian-Tory
contingent that had joined his army. He had hoped for a force
of a thousand or more, but only 250 showed up. This puny
figure seemed to indicate that a number of sympathizers preferred to sit on the sidelines, waiting to see which side was going
to have the best of it before they committed themselves—a
timorous attitude that kept an estimated one third of the pop-
ulation of the rebelling colonies fence-sitting throughout the
Revolution.

The Indians turned out in larger numbers than the Tories.
There were 400 of them, and they were under the command of
two unsavory Canadians, Louis St. Luc de la Corne and Charles
de Langlade. Both had been noted for atrocities committed by
Indians under their command on the British themselves during
the French and Indian War, but now Burgoyne welcomed them
and hoped to make use of them against the American rebels.

Gentleman Johnny's conscience disturbed him, however, and
so he addressed his savage allies in one of the most ridiculous
speeches man ever penned. It was so bombastic, so determinedly
blind to the realities of Indian warfare, that it made Burgoyne a
laughingstock on both sides of the Atlantic.

Speaking of King George III as the great father of all, including the Indians, Burgoyne took off in this flight of flowery
verbiage:

"The clemency of your father has been abused, the offers of
his mercy have been despised, and his farther patience would, in

his eyes, become culpable, in as much as it would with-hold redress from the most grievous oppressions in the provinces that ever disgraced the history of mankind . . . Warriors, you are free—go forth in might and valour of your cause—strike at the common enemies of Great Britain and America, disturbers of the public order, peace and happiness, destroyers of commerce, parricides of state."

But the noble warriors, while striking, were to be gentlemanly about it. Burgoyne told them:

"I positively forbid bloodshed, when you are not opposed in arms.

"Aged men, women, children, and prisoners must be held sacred from the knife or hatchet, even in the time of actual conflict.

"You shall receive compensation for the prisoners you take, but you shall be called to account for your scalps."

Scalps were to be taken only from enemies killed honorably on the battlefield.

When Burgoyne finished his speech, the Indians cried: "Etow! Etow!" It was their way of saying, "Hurrah! Hurrah!"

Rum was then issued, a liquor that always sent the susceptible Indians into a frenzy, and the warriors performed a wild war dance, "every now and then making the most hideous yells."

Frances Hopkinson, the American patriot, wrote a long and much-quoted poem, parroting and ridiculing Burgoyne for speaking of "clemency" and "mercy" on the one hand—and on the other, employing bloodthirsty Indians, who had never hesitated to brain and scalp the helpless, as the instruments of this "mercy." In England, Horace Walpole called the general "the vaporing Burgoyne" and "Pomposo," and he marveled that one who spoke with the "consciousness of Christianity" could "reconcile the scalping knife with the Gospel . . ."

The most devastating oratorical blow of all was delivered by the great Edmund Burke, friend of the colonists and an opponent of the war. Speaking in the House of Commons, Burke ridiculed Burgoyne's appeal to the Indians to make war as perfect, red-skinned gentlemen by imagining the scene that might take place if wild animals were let loose from His Majesty's zoo.

"Suppose there was a riot on Tower Hill," he said. "What would the keeper of his Majesty's lions do? Would he not fling open the dens of the wild beasts and then address them thus: 'My gentle lions—my human bears—my tenderhearted hyenas, go forth! But I exhort you, as you are Christians and members of civil society, to take care not to harm any man, woman or child.'"

According to Horace Walpole, Burke's parody was so effective that even Prime Minister North, a man not much given to humor, laughed until the tears rolled down his cheeks. But it was to be, in the end, no laughing matter. This resort to Indian warfare, which Carleton had opposed, and Burgoyne's farcical attempt to cloak it with trappings of humanity would combine to rouse an entire countryside against Burgoyne's version of His Majesty's "clemency" and "mercy."

CHAPTER FIVE

Ticonderoga Falls

THE BRITISH FLOTILLA swept majestically down Lake Champlain, and on June 21 all segments of the army, after assembling at Cumberland Head just north of Valcour Island, set out into the broader reaches of the lake. Lieutenant Thomas Anburey, a grenadier officer who kept a diary, described the colorful spectacle. First went the Indians, painted every color from green to blood red, "their birch-bark canoes containing twenty to thirty men each." The advanced corps followed "in regular line with the gun-boats." Next came "the *Royal George* and *Inflexible*, towing large booms—which are to be thrown across two points of land—with two brigs and sloops following." The armada swelled out across the lake, the waters mirroring the scarlet coats of British regulars, the blue uniforms of the Hessians and Brunswickers, the light green of the jägers, the riflemen of the army. It all formed, in Anburey's words, "the most complete and splendid regatta you can possibly conceive."

So powerful was the British fleet, manned by some 700 officers and men of the Royal Navy, that there was no opposition. American power on the lake had been expended at Valcour Island the year before, and the British vessels sailed irresistibly onward, their canvas billowed by the breezes that swept down from the heights of the Adirondacks. General Simon Fraser, who commanded the advance corps, reached Crown Point on June 26, then started south to scout the defenses of that so-called "Gibraltar of the North"—Fort Ticonderoga.

What about this famous fort? Was it really the Gibraltar that the Americans believed it to be?

Ticonderoga was strategically placed to command the strait between Lake George and Lake Champlain. As one went north, Lake George narrowed into a small creek which eventually made a right-angled bend and flowed to the east. At a tapering point of land jutting out from the New York shore, the waters made a left-hand bend and flowed north into Lake Champlain. Precisely at this spot where the two lakes merged, a little point of land stuck out from the eastern, or Vermont, shore, creating a narrows no more than a quarter of a mile wide. The Indian name, Ticonderoga, meant the place "where the lake shuts itself," and it was obvious that a fort, situated to command this water gap, could bar passage of hostile forces up and down the chain of lakes.

Fort Ticonderoga had become, as a result, the most fought-over military bastion in the thirteen colonies. The French had thrown up the first crude earthworks in 1690. In 1750 they built a powerful stone fortress on the New York tongue of land, and they named it the Carillon after the caroling of the waters. They added horseshoe-shaped earthworks to protect the fort itself from assault from the northwest, making Ticonderoga formidable indeed. Throughout the French and Indian War it was fought over the way hostile dogs quarrel over a tasty bone. One British-Colonial army led by General James Abercrombie battered its head against the strong walls with an appalling loss of life, and it was not until the closing days of the war that a force led by Lord Jeffrey Amherst finally conquered Ticonderoga.

Ethan Allen and Benedict Arnold had seized the stronghold in a surprise night raid at the outset of the Revolution. Ever since, the American patriots had regarded Ticonderoga as their insurance against invasion from the north. They had added to its fortifications. Along the eastward-running rivulet coming from

Lake George, they had built an outpost which they named Mount Hope and which was designed to protect an important sawmill. Directly across from Ticonderoga itself, on the point of land on the Vermont side of the narrows, they had constructed another fort that they called Mount Independence.

On paper these battlements, so strategically located, appeared as impregnable as Gibraltar. But they had basic and fatal weaknesses.

For one thing, the Americans, by extending their lines and building more forts, had created a situation that demanded ever more manpower. It was estimated that a good 12,000 troops would be needed to man all these defenses—and the northern army never had more than a fraction of that number of effective soldiers.

A second weakness was even more glaring. The fortifications of Ticonderoga were overlooked—indeed, dominated—by a sugar-loaf hill some 800 feet high to the southwest. It was later to be named Mount Defiance. Throughout the French and Indian War, despite all the fighting that had raged around the fort, none of the commanders had paid much attention to Mount Defiance. They appear to have assumed that its sides were too steep for men to scale and place cannon upon the summit.

In the summer of 1776, however, John Trumbull, though only twenty, looked at Mount Defiance with his artist's eyes, noticing the manner in which it seemed to loom over Ticonderoga. He expressed the thought that the fort might lie at the mercy of anyone who could place artillery on top of that sugar-loaf hill, but he was laughed at for his fears.

Trumbull was obstinate, however, and he got the permission of Horatio Gates to make a test. A twelve-pounder with a double charge of powder was fired from Mount Independence on the Vermont shore, and the ball struck halfway up the slope of Mount Defiance. Then a six-pounder was fired from Ticonderoga itself, and the ball nearly reached the summit.

The demonstration proved how vulnerable the fort was to any enemy who dragged cannon up Mount Defiance. But could this be done? Trumbull, accompanied by "Mad Anthony" Wayne and Benedict Arnold, clambered up the steep eastern face of the mount and reached the summit. They discovered that the northern slope was more gradual, and they became convinced that cannon could be dragged up it. Despite this, no defenses were constructed on Mount Defiance.

The reasons for this failure to act on the obvious were many. For one thing, the garrison of Fort Ticonderoga was totally inadequate and in deplorable straits. For another, Congress wavered back and forth between Gates and Schuyler, creating a chaos in the command structure. In mid-November 1776, Gates threw up his command of Ticonderoga and dashed off to plead his case before Congress, doing his utmost to cut Schuyler's throat. Behind him, he left Mad Anthony Wayne in command at Ticonderoga.

Wayne's description of the conditions that existed at the time was graphic. The place, he wrote, "appears to be the last part of the world that God made, and I have some ground to believe it was finished in the dark." The ground around the fort was littered with the skulls and bones of Abercrombie's men. The skulls, Wayne wrote, "are so plentiful here that our people for want of other vessels drink out of them, whilst the soldiers make tent pins of the shin and thigh bones of Abercrombie's men."

There were only 1700 men to garrison defenses that needed 12,000—and, of these 1700, one third lacked shoes in the sub-zero northern winter. Food was scarce, and men sickened and died. Wayne described this scene: "I paid a visit to the sick yesterday, in a small house called a hospital. The first object presented to my eyes, one man lying dead at the door, the inside two more lying dead, two living lying between them: the living with the dead had so lain for twenty-four hours."

It might have been expected that this fort of horrors would have claimed the attention and energy of its true commander, Horatio Gates, but Gates was more interested in his own career than in the desperate situation he left behind him. He was galled at the thought that he, a professional soldier, must play second fiddle to the amateur warrior Philip Schuyler; and Schuyler's wealth, his patrician air, his courtly gentlemanliness grated on a man who was abnormally sensitive about his own common birth and who was negligent, almost slovenly in his dress as if to express his contempt for the genteel. Gates simply could not stand the thought of serving under Schuyler, and so he hurried south to Baltimore, where the Continental Congress was then temporarily sitting. There he found allies among the New Englanders, who disliked Schuyler for his aristocratic bearing (some even questioned his patriotism) and for the strict discipline he sought to impose on his troops. In these circumstances, Gates intrigued so successfully that he induced Congress to name him the supreme commander in the North.

Schuyler, learning that he had been superseded, erupted in a roar of outrage and hurried south in his turn. The Continental Congress had returned to Philadelphia, and Schuyler appeared before it and demanded that his authority be restored. He had been humiliated and disgraced, he said, and Congress must right the wrong—or else. Faced with his angry determination and the loss of his services if it stuck by Gates, the Congress yielded, again reversed itself, and on May 22, 1777, reappointed Schuyler to the command of the entire Northern Department, including Ticonderoga.

The Gates-Schuyler vendetta had wasted all kinds of precious time and had left the forces in the North almost leaderless at the very instant the British were ready to pounce. Burgoyne's army was already starting down the lake before the Americans could decide who should command what. Schuyler selected Major General Arthur St. Clair, a former British Army officer, to take over command at Ticonderoga, but St. Clair did not even reach the fort until June 12. Schuyler himself arrived a week later, and they held a council of war.

Some reinforcements had arrived, but the garrison was still woefully weak. St. Clair had some 3000 men under his command, 2000 of them regulars, the rest militia. As had been the case since the previous year, many were barefoot, all were ragged, and supplies were too sparse to withstand a long siege. Appalled, Schuyler reported that conditions were worse than he could possibly have imagined, and he held out little hope for a successful defense if the British came in force. His one hope was that they would not; for except for the ragtag garrison at Ticonderoga, he had no army. There were only 700 other soldiers under his command in the entire Northern Department.

This was the desperate state of affairs when, on June 30, just eleven days after the Schuyler-St. Clair council of war, the British invasion fleet hove into view. Preceded by gunboats and two warships, some 200 bateaux and a host of lesser craft swept down the lake, wheeled just three miles north of Ticonderoga, and began to pour troops ashore on both the New York and Vermont shores. "We are now within sight of the enemy," Anburey wrote. "We are now arrived before a place that is more talked of in this war than the last."

The British fanned out around the American fortifications, and it was not long before they spotted the Achilles' heel of Fort Ticonderoga—that sugar-loaf summit called Mount Defiance that overlooked all the American works. "Where a goat can go, a man can go, and where a man can go, he can drag a gun," declared British Major General William Phillips, studying Mount Defiance.

On July 5 Phillips sent out a fatigue party to clear a path up the northern slope, and by nightfall two cannon from Burgoyne's massive artillery train had been hauled up to the summit and placed overlooking the American lines. The feat should have enabled the British to take the Americans completely by surprise, but the effect of surprise was lost by two blunders. Burgoyne's Indians could not refrain from lighting fires on the summit of the hill, and an overeager gunner fired one of the cannon at a vessel in the narrows.

General St. Clair, hearing the firing, turned to an aide, Colonel James Wilkinson, and remarked: "We must away from this, for our situation has become desperate."

He realized that Fort Ticonderoga could be quickly pounded into submission as soon as the British dragged a full battery up to the summit of Mount Defiance. The important thing now was to save his army—the only army that existed in the North.

 *Escape*

ON A BEAUTIFUL clear night, with a full moon shining brilliantly upon the scene, General St. Clair and his little army stole away under the noses of Burgoyne and the British. The Americans' escape route lay across the quarter-mile water gap separating Fort Ticonderoga from Mount Independence. With infinite labor in the preceding months, they had tried to bar this channel to Burgoyne's warships by building a heavy boom across it. Alongside this boom, they had constructed a floating bridge, across which the Ticonderoga garrison now made its way to the eastern shore of the lake.

To cover the movement, St. Clair had the guns of the fort banging away at the British throughout the night. It is not quite clear what the British thought of this, if indeed they thought anything. Such a cannonade was a sheer waste of powder and ball since the chances of hitting even a British mule were minimal; but Burgoyne, perhaps amusing himself with his mistress, whose husband had been left conveniently behind in Canada, seems not to have wondered what might be happening.

The American retreat was so sudden, so unexpected, and so swift that it caught some of the Americans themselves by surprise. Dr. James Thacher, the medical officer at Ticonderoga, recorded in his journal how, about midnight on July 5, "I was urgently called from sleep, and informed that our army was in motion, and was instantly to abandon Fort Ticonderoga and Mount Independence. I could scarcely believe that my informant was in earnest . . ."

Dr. Thacher hastily bundled up what medical supplies could be carried away and got his sick and wounded aboard the little squadron of galleys, schooners, and bateaux—the remnants of Arnold's 1776 fleet—that had been anchored across the channel on the south side of the heavy boom and floating bridge. A narrow prong of Lake Champlain extended straight to the south, east of the longer and deeper waters of Lake George. This stream led to nowhere, ending in the deep wilderness at the little hamlet of Skenesborough. It offered, however, the best escape route for those too sick and weak to march; and so St. Clair sent Dr. Thacher and his patients down this inviting waterway. The rest of his army trudged by a circuitous route along the east side of the lake, hoping to join them.

Secrecy was essential if the ragged Continentals and militia were to get a good head start from British pursuit, but all kinds of blunders now helped to alert even the slumbering British to what was happening. The French adventurer General Roche de Fermoy had been given command of American forces on Mount Independence; and when the retreat began, he set fire to his headquarters, touching off a blaze that lit the landscape for miles around and made the British wonder whether the Americans "were meditating an attack or . . . were retreating."

British uncertainty was quickly set to rest when, early in the morning of July 6, three American deserters came into Burgoyne's camp and informed him of the retreat. General Simon Fraser, commanding the advance corps on the west side of the lake, moved swiftly and hoisted the British colors above Fort Ticonderoga as the dawn broke. On the opposite side of the lake, Baron von Riedesel with his German troops set out in pursuit, swiftly joined and soon outdistanced by Fraser's men pouring over the floating bridge.

The Americans had attempted to burn the bridge, but had

succeeded only in pitting it with some black, charred holes around which the British stepped warily. Loaded cannon had been placed at the eastern end of the bridge, and four American cannoneers had been left there with instructions to fire one deadly blast into the packed British ranks as they crossed. But the cannon were never fired. Anburey, the British diarist, explained that the four Americans, "allured by the sweets of plunder and liquor," had broached a keg of madeira and had sampled its contents to such good effect that they were stretched out dead drunk beside their cannon, their lighted matches beside them. Even so, the British had a narrow escape. One of Burgoyne's Indians, prowling with the advance, came upon the glowing matches beside the cannon. "As he was very curious in examining everything that came his way," Anburey wrote, "he took up the match that lay on the ground, with some fire remaining in it, when a spark dropping upon the pinning of the cannon, it went off, loaded with all manner of combustibles, but it fortunately happened that the gun was so elevated that no mischief was done."

Fraser's troops, unscathed and unopposed, raced across the bridge and took up the pursuit. Behind them, Burgoyne ordered his fleet to smash through the boom and bridge and chase Dr. Thacher's detachment down the lake. The Americans had expected the boom to delay the British for hours. But Burgoyne's vessels, with a strong north wind behind them, came bowling down the lake with such speed and force that they smashed through the links of the boom in half an hour and sped on south toward Skenesborough.

Colonel Pierce Long of New Hampshire, with some 400 troops, had escorted Dr. Thacher's patients to this wilderness outpost, and they were all congratulating themselves on having gotten safely away when, about five o'clock in the afternoon, without warning, Burgoyne's pursuing forces pounced upon them. Dr. Thacher wrote that "we were struck with surprise and consternation by a discharge of cannon from the enemy's fleet on our gallies and batteaux lying at the wharf . . . It was not long before it was perceived that a number of their troops

and savages had landed and were rapidly advancing towards
our little party. The officers of our guard now attempted to rally
the men and form them in battle array; but this was found
impossible, every effort proved unavailing, and in the utmost
panic they were seen to fly in every direction for personal safety."

The refugees fled south through the woods to Fort Anne on
Wood Creek to the east of the southern tip of Lake George.
They were closely pursued by the British, but after a night-long
flight through the forests, about five o'clock the following morning, the exhausted survivors staggered into the fort. They had
lost almost everything. As Dr. Thacher wrote, all their cannon
and provisions, "the bulk of our baggage, with several invalids,
fell into the enemy's hands."

The main body of St. Clair's forces was having an equally
difficult time. This detachment hurried to the south and east,
inland toward Hubbardton, Vermont, hoping to outdistance the
British pursuit and circle around Burgoyne's troops to join up
with the Skenesborough party and whatever forces Schuyler
could muster. The "road" that they followed to Hubbardton
was a mere wilderness trace, a narrow wagon track, rough,
rutted, spotted with the stumps of trees. Dense walls of forest
closed in above the road, cutting off any wandering breezes,
and the broiling sun turned the trail into an oven. Sweltering
and exhausted, the fleeing troops kept going at a rapid pace for
twenty-four miles until they came through a high notch in the
hills to Hubbardton, a hamlet with just two houses.

Even then, St. Clair would not let them pause. He pushed his
panting soldiers to the outer limits of their endurance, marching
them another six miles to Castleton. Here they were only thirteen or fourteen miles from Skenesborough, and here at last
they collapsed for the night.

St. Clair had left a force behind him at Hubbardton to protect his rear. Colonel Seth Warner, with his Vermont regiment
of 173 Green Mountain Boys, was in command. With him was
Colonel Nathan Hale (no relation to the famous American spy
of the same name) with a New Hampshire regiment of about
360 men. Their instructions were to await the arrival of St.

Clair's rear guard, composed of 420 Massachusetts Continentals under Colonel Ebenezer Francis—then to hurry on and join the rest of the army.

When Francis arrived about four o'clock on the afternoon of July 6, however, the three colonels held a conference and decided to camp at Hubbardton for the night. There were probably two reasons for this decision: the exhausted condition of the men after the long forced march in sweltering heat and the belief that they had outdistanced the enemy and were safe for the moment from pursuit. In this, they were greatly mistaken.

Simon Fraser was undoubtedly the best field commander Burgoyne had. When he took up the pursuit, he didn't give his men time even to eat, collect rations, or fill their canteens; he pushed them forward as fast and as furiously as the men could march. Behind him, Riedesel whipped on his more heavily encumbered German troops. In late afternoon, Riedesel rode ahead of his main body, and the two generals conferred. Fraser had been picking up American stragglers, and he knew he was not far behind St. Clair's rear guard. But his men were exhausted. He and Riedesel decided, therefore, that they would camp for the night, but they would put their forces in motion at three o'clock the next morning and try to catch the Americans by surprise.

Their plan worked almost to perfection. The Americans had stationed only a single sentry to keep watch—and the Indians captured him. With no lookout, there was no warning. Hale's New Hampshire troops were sitting at breakfast around their campfires when, shortly before sunrise, the British charged upon them. "The enemy is upon us," someone cried—and panic followed. Hale and his men fled into the woods.

The sound of scattered firing alerted Warner and Francis. Warner's Green Mountain Boys, taking cover behind fallen trees, fired into the advancing British, killing some twenty men, including a major. Colonel Francis and his Massachusetts Continentals held the strongest position on the half-mile American front, a high hill on which a man named Sellick had built a cabin, with some cleared farmland around it. Francis and Warner were conferring at the cabin when a courier from St. Clair dashed up with disastrous news—the word that the British had broken through the boom and bridge and had already reached Skenesborough. St. Clair informed the two colonels that, as a result, he was going to have to make a wider detour, circling east all the way to Rutland in Vermont to get around the British and then turning west to join Schuyler, who was at Fort Edward, twenty-five miles south of Skenesborough. It now became more urgent than ever for the surprised and almost-trapped American rear guard to keep the road to Castleton open if it was to have a chance of rejoining St. Clair.

Colonel Francis swung his Massachusetts Continentals into line along the crest of the ridge that was later to be named Monument Hill. The British advance, led by the Earl of Balcarres, stormed up the slope, but the Americans poured such a deadly fire upon them that they broke ranks and fled. Twenty-one men in the leading platoon had been killed or wounded. Balcarres himself had taken a ball through one arm and later counted thirty bullet holes in his jacket.

Their attack blunted for the moment, the British now took advantage of a weakness in the American defense. A high, precipitous hill known as Mount Zion overlooked the whole battlefield. It had been left unoccupied, and the British now seized it, scrambling almost straight up into the sky, bracing their feet on rocks, clutching at roots to pull themselves upward, in danger any moment of losing their grip and being dashed to death on the rocks below. Once they had gained the summit, they overlooked the vital Castleton Road and could sweep it with their fire.

Still the gallant Colonel Francis and his men stuck to their position on Monument Hill. Balcarres tried to storm their line again, but Francis threw his men down the hill in a surprise counterattack. The Americans poured another volley of point-blank fire into the packed British ranks. Another ball grazed Balcarres' shoulder, one of his officers was killed; and on the American side, Colonel Francis' right arm was shattered by a bullet. Again the British broke and tumbled back down the hill, and the Americans returned to their line on the crest.

The welling sounds of battle now summoned reinforcements from both sides. St. Clair sent detachments back to help his embattled rear guard, but they were too far away to arrive in time. Riedesel was closer. He had put his men on the road at 3 A.M. as he had promised Fraser; and, capable commander that he was, he spurred ahead with 180 jägers and grenadiers as the sounds of battle told him of Fraser's desperate need. The German reinforcements came on the field at a crucial moment. Balcarres was just launching his third attack against the Americans on Monument Hill. Colonel Francis, leaping to the front and calling upon his men for one more good volley, fell dead, shot through the heart by a German rifle bullet. His men, deprived of their leader, gave way.

With Riedesel on the field, further resistance was useless, and Warner's Green Mountain Boys and Francis' Continentals scattered and melted into the woods. The furious action had lasted an hour and three quarters, and the casualties on both sides were heavy. The Americans lost 96 killed and wounded and 228 taken prisoner, most of these members of Hale's regiment who surrendered with their commander after milling around in the woods and doing virtually no fighting. On the British side, Fraser lost 50 killed and 100 wounded out of a force of 850 men; even Riedesel's late-arriving Germans had 10 killed and 14 wounded. Casualties were especially heavy among the British officers. Fraser lost two officers killed and sixteen wounded, a tribute to American marksmanship and a foretaste of things to come.

Fraser had won the battle but had exhausted himself in winning it. He was burdened with prisoners and wounded, his men battle weary; and so he had to pause where he was, giving up the pursuit. As one of Burgoyne's officers remarked, "the Advance Corps certainly discovered that neither were they invincible, nor the Rebels all Poltroons." The Americans had fought with desperate courage and in the end had gotten clean away, to fight with equal fury on other battlefields on other days. And the British had begun the long drain on their manpower; they had started to lose men they could not replace.

None of this was obvious at the time. On both sides of the Atlantic, only one fact registered: Fort Ticonderoga, the Gibraltar of the North, had fallen almost without a shot—and the Americans were in panicked flight. It seemed, at the moment, almost like the end of everything.

"The abandonment of Fort Ticonderoga and Mount Independence has occasioned the greatest surprise and alarm," Dr. Thacher wrote in his journal. "No event could be more unexpected nor more severely felt throughout our army and country."

Dr. Thacher put it mildly. George Washington was so shocked that he called the fall of Ticonderoga an event "not within the compass of my reasoning." John Adams was so enraged that he wrote his wife, Abigail, "I think we shall never defend a post until we shoot a general." New Englanders, who had always distrusted Schuyler, were convinced that he and St. Clair were both traitors, and for months they circulated the fantastic story of the silver balls.

As Dr. Thacher noted: "It has been industriously reported that Generals Schuyler and St. Clair acted the part of traitors to their country and that they were paid for their treason by the enemy in *silver balls* shot from Burgoyne's guns into our camp and that they were collected by the order of General St. Clair and divided between him and General Schuyler."

On the British side, Burgoyne's great stroke in seizing Ticonderoga so easily raised the most exaggerated hopes of total victory. When Burgoyne's report reached London on August 22, official circles went wild with rejoicing. King George III, believing he had won the entire war, capered into the Queen's bedroom, crying: "I have beat them, I have beat all the Americans."

Few at the time recognized that St. Clair, by his wise and sudden abandonment of the fort, by his forced-march retreat, had accomplished the supreme feat: he had kept an army in the North in being; he had saved a core of fighting men around whom a whole countryside could rally. Only young Alexander

Hamilton, then on Washington's staff, appears to have seen the situation clearly. On July 13 he wrote:

". . . If the army gets off safe, we shall soon be able to recover the face of affairs. I am in hope that Burgoyne's success will precipitate him into measures that will prove his ruin. The enterprising spirit he has credit for, I suspect, may easily be fanned by his vanity into rashness."

It was as if Hamilton were looking into a crystal ball and reading the future.

CHAPTER SEVEN

Burgoyne, Gates, and Jane McCrea

THE CAMPAIGN now turned upon human factors, upon the strengths and flaws of the incredible cast of characters who were to make Saratoga so memorable. Gentleman Johnny Burgoyne charged south with the main body of his army, reaching Skenesborough on July 9—and there he sat. He had scored such a remarkable opening victory that he may well have believed the campaign all but won. In just ten days, he had captured the Americans' most powerful fortress and had seized a flotilla of some 200 vessels of all sizes, some 100 cannon, and quantities of stores, powder, and shot. He was only twenty-three miles from Fort Edward at the headwaters of the Hudson River, only seventy-five miles from Albany itself. Only a paper-thin screen of disorganized rebel forces stood in his way. It seemed an occasion for celebration, and Gentleman Johnny, never loath, celebrated.

The hamlet of Skenesborough was named after Philip Skene, a former British Army major. Skene had been a professional soldier for thirty years. He had been wounded in 1758 during Abercrombie's assault on Ticonderoga; he had been with Amherst the following year when the fort was taken. After the war, he had acquired a huge tract of wilderness property on Wood

Creek, a rivulet running into the lower prong of Lake Champlain. There he had built a handsome yellow fieldstone mansion, a sawmill, a forge, and other facilities. In this mansion, in the flush of first success, Gentleman Johnny installed himself and his mistress. The thirty carts carrying his belongings, her baggage, and—most important of all—his vast cargo of wines caught up with them, making life enjoyable. Gentleman Johnny gave General Riedesel four dozen bottles of port and an equal number of madeira, grumbling a bit about the quality of the latter; and he launched upon a round of high living that became noted in the traditions of Skenesborough.

In the meantime, the war that could not wait—wars can never wait—waited. It seems obvious that Burgoyne should have thrown forward Simon Fraser's elite advance corps, traveling fast and light, to harass the disorganized, dispirited patriot forces. But he did not. He sat and deliberated on his next move.

He had two choices, and it was perhaps the evil genius of his campaign, Philip Skene himself, who impelled him to make the wrong one. Skene had joined the Tories at the outset of the Revolution; he had gone to Canada and become a colonel. He was the eternal conservative optimist. It seemed incredible to him that a scruffy band of rebels could successfully oppose the King's authority; certainly the great bulk of the people could not possibly side with such riffraff. He was constantly telling Burgoyne that the whole countryside would rise to join him at any moment. And, when it came to a selection of the invasion route south, Philip Skene had a personal interest.

Twenty-three miles of almost impenetrable forest, creeks, and swamps separated Skene's holdings from their best commercial outlet to the south, the Hudson River at Fort Edward. A road built through this wilderness tract would be invaluable to him when the war ended in a British victory, as of course it must, and when all his lands and possessions would be restored to him. As a result, Skene is believed to have urged upon Burgoyne that he should slash straight south through the wilderness to Fort Edward.

The irony is that Burgoyne himself, in outlining his campaign plans back in London, had considered and discarded this route. He had written that there were two avenues of attack from Ticonderoga, one by way of Lake Champlain, Wood Creek, and Skenesborough; the other down Lake George. The Lake George way, he wrote, was "the most expeditious and most commodious route to Albany." At the end of Lake George his forces would have to penetrate only ten miles of wilderness to reach the Hudson.

On the other hand, Burgoyne had foreseen the enormous hazards and difficulties of the Skenesborough route. The wilderness area south of Skenesborough was known as "the drowned lands." Numerous creeks and streams threaded through it; the ground was low and marshy. "The narrow parts of the river [Wood Creek] may easily be choked up and rendered impassable, and at best there will be a necessity for a great deal of land carriage for the artillery, provisions, etc.," Burgoyne had written. He had foreseen that the Americans would "take measures to close the road from Ticonderoga to Albany by way of Skenesborough, and by felling trees, breaking bridges, and other obvious impediments," they could put gigantic obstacles in his way if he chose that route.

Despite all this, he now chose it. His justification later was that, if he had taken the Lake George passage, he would have had to retreat to Ticonderoga, a move that he thought might damage the morale of his army and "abate the panic of the enemy." Gentleman Johnny, the dashing cavalryman, apparently could not understand that there are moments in war when a strategic retreat is the wiser course; and his obstinacy, his refusal to recognize this fact, was to plague him throughout the campaign and lead him to his final, irretrievable blunders.

It was not so with Philip Schuyler, still his adversary. The much-maligned, aristocratic Schuyler was no dashing Benedict Arnold in the field; but all of the evidence says he had many of the qualities of an excellent headquarters commander in chief. He was a fine administrator, and he had a broad strategic vision.

The fall of Ticonderoga had thrown him into a momentary blue funk. He found himself in command of an army that was

little more than a disorganized rabble. For days, he did not
know what had happened to St. Clair, and it was not until
June 12 that this worry was relieved when St. Clair, after his
long circuitous march, joined up with him.

Schuyler's letters to Washington, which were forwarded to
Congress, painted the blackest picture and rang with overtones
of despair. His description of the circumstances he faced was
factual enough, but New England politicians, who had never
liked or trusted him, became convinced that he was a timorous
defeatist and that there was no hope of success as long as he was
in command of the northern army. In this, as usual, they greatly
underestimated and wronged Schuyler.

For while Burgoyne frolicked at Skenesborough, deciding on
his next step, Schuyler did just what Burgoyne himself had predicted a good general would do. He sent 1000 axmen into the
virgin forest to hack down huge trees. The British forces at
Skenesborough heard the thud of their axes ringing day and
night. Giant pines and other trees were felled across the rutted
wilderness trail, their branches interlacing to form barriers that
could not be dragged away. Huge mountain boulders were rolled
into streams and more trees felled, creating wood-and-rock dams
that trapped the flowing waters, turning swamps into lakes and
creating vast new bogs. Schuyler's couriers ranged far and wide
across the countryside, warning the inhabitants to flee with their
cattle and livestock and to burn crops that could not be carried
away. It was a "scorched-earth" policy that led one American
observer to write: "It seems a maxim with General Schuyler to
leave no support to the enemy as he retires. All is devastation
and waste when he leaves. By this means the enemy will not be
able to pursue as fast as they could wish."

Instead of sending out raiders to interfere with this campaign
of obstruction, Burgoyne dispatched his own corps of axmen to
hack through the barriers Schuyler had so skillfully erected. His
ponderous artillery train he sent by the way of Lake George, but
for sixteen insufferable days his working parties slashed their
way painfully through the wilderness wall Schuyler had put in
their path. Swarms of gnats and mosquitoes almost nibbled them

to death; the muggy heat brought many almost to the point of collapse as they inched painfully forward. As Burgoyne himself later described it: "The troops had not only layers of these [trees] to remove, in places where it was impossible to take any other direction, but also they had above forty bridges to construct and others to repair, one of which was of log-work over a morass two miles in extent."

After his work parties had cleared a track, Burgoyne's army crawled slowly forward, reaching the Hudson at Fort Edward on July 29. He had been delayed for more than three weeks, time he could not afford to lose and would never regain; and he had crept forward after his first impressive victories at a rate of only about one mile a day.

Though time favored the Americans, they were still in a desperate state. Schuyler's Continentals were quitting when their time was up; the militia had not rallied in force, and even some who had come in were deserting. Schuyler had what one of his captains called "this retreating, ragged, starved, lousy, thievish, pockey army." Unable to fight Burgoyne, he abandoned weak Fort Edward and fell back, first to Saratoga, then to Stillwater. He wrote Washington frantic appeals for aid; and Washington, in hard straits himself, had little to give. It seemed as if the whole patriot cause was about to collapse unless it received, out of the blue, some powerful shot in the arm—and just now, in the moment of ultimate despair, it did.

Burgoyne's Indian marauders supplied the necessary spark. They ranged in advance of the army during the slow crawl to Fort Edward. They reached Fort Edward on July 27, two days ahead of Burgoyne. They slaughtered the entire family of John Allen—himself, his wife, three children, and three Negro slaves. And then, on this same fateful day, they scalped Jane McCrea.

Jane, the daughter of a New Jersey Presbyterian minister, had been living with her brother, John, a lawyer, at his home on Moses Kill, a tributary of the Hudson. John, a colonel in the local militia, had gone off to join Schuyler. But Jane, a Tory, was in love with David Jones of Fort Edward, a Tory who was now a lieutenant in Burgoyne's approaching army. Anxious to join her lover, she had gone forward to Fort Edward, where she stayed with a Mrs. McNeil, an enormously fat widow who was, by chance, a cousin of the British General Simon Fraser.

Jane McCrea, who was to become a heroine of tragic legend, was just twenty-three years old. Descriptions of her do not agree; many, doubtless, exaggerate. She was described variously as "tall and noted for her long lustrous hair, which could reach to the floor when she stood up and let it down"; as "so lovely in disposition, so graceful in manners and so intelligent in features, that she was a favorite with all who knew her"; as having hair "darker than a raven's wing"; as having "clustering curls of soft blonde hair"; as "finely formed, dark hair and uncommonly beautiful."

Whether her hair was blond or dark, everyone agreed that it was a shining glory, and the Jane McCrea of popular imagination became an almost incredibly perfect and marvelous young woman. The legend began soon after she and Mrs. McNeil were dragged out of their cabin by raiding Indians on this July 27.

What really happened remains a mystery. According to one account, the Indians seized two horses and started back to the British camp with their prisoners. Jane was boosted up on the back of one horse, but the corpulent Mrs. McNeil was too heavy to hoist on the other. In disgust, it seems, the Indians stripped Mrs. McNeil naked and had her trudging along in the dust behind them. Somehow, as a result, the two women became separated on the trail, and there were no eyewitnesses to Jane McCrea's death.

All that is known is that in the evening the Indians reached the British camp, flourishing two bloody trophies. And one of these was a scalp with such beautiful and distinctively long tresses that Lieutenant David Jones instantly recognized it as that of his beloved. The reaction in the British camp is perhaps best capsuled in this entry from the journal of Lieutenant William Digby of the Shropshire Regiment:

"In the evening, our Indians brought in two scalps, one of them an officer's which they danced about in their usual manner.

Indeed, the cruelties committed by them are too shocking to relate, particularly the melancholy catastrophe of the unfortunate Miss McCrea, which affected the general and the whole army with the sincerest regret and concern for her untimely fate. This young lady was about 18, had a pleasing person, her family were loyal to the King, and she engaged to be married to a provincial officer in our army before the war broke out. Our Indians (I may well now call them Savages) were detached in scouting parties, both in our front and on our flanks, and came to the house where she resided; but the scene is too tragic for my pen. She fell a sacrifice to the savage passions of these blood thirsty monsters . . ."

Wyandot Panther, who had been flourishing the girl's scalp, argued that she had been shot accidentally by the Americans themselves. In firing at his party, he said, some Americans had aimed too high and shot Jane upon her horse; then, naturally, he had taken her scalp. Neither Burgoyne nor anyone else in the British camp believed him. Gentleman Johnny went to the Indian encampment and insisted that Wyandot Panther be turned over to him for trial and execution. St. Luc de la Corne, the renegade leader of the Indians, faced down the general and warned that if he carried out his threat, every Indian with the army would desert. Burgoyne blustered that he "would rather lose every Indian in his army than connive at their enormities," but in the end he backtracked after getting a promise that the Indians would be better "children" in the future.

It was a compromise that gained him nothing and cost him much. Burgoyne's threat against Wyandot Panther did almost as much damage as the execution of that scalper would have done; the Indians, insulted, decamped the next day loaded with their plunder and scalps. Burgoyne was left with only about 50 of the 500 Indians he had had after some new Indian recruits had joined him at Skenesborough.

He also suffered another telling desertion. Lieutenant David Jones, having recovered the beautiful tresses of his loved one from Wyandot Panther, asked to leave the army. When Burgoyne refused, he simply deserted and went back to Canada, where he buried himself in the deep woods, which, according to his grandniece many years later, "he had never been known to leave, except upon one mysterious occasion . . ."

Such was the story that created for the Americans the image of a wilderness Joan of Arc. It was a story made to order for propaganda—and so for the purposes of the master schemer who now became commander in chief of the American army in the North.

Horatio Gates, whom Burgoyne was to call "that old midwife," never demonstrated, as Benedict Arnold and Daniel Morgan did, any passion for placing himself where the bullets flew thickest; but when it came to intrigue, he was a master. At Boston he had shuddered at the daring idea of placing guns on Dorchester Heights to drive the British out, a tactic that had worked to perfection. After joining Washington just before the Battle of Trenton, he had begged off from the fight. Washington had wanted him to command the right wing of the army in the attack across the Delaware; but Gates sent his rascally aide, James Wilkinson, to inform his commander that he was just too ill for such hazardous duty and needed to go to Philadelphia to regain his health. Instead, he went off to Baltimore and engaged in his first successful intrigue with the Continental Congress to supersede Schuyler.

After Schuyler got this action reversed, he offered Gates the command of Ticonderoga; but to Gates, his own career was more important than the war. He threw up his command and hurried off to Philadelphia to intrigue with Congress again. The impression that he made on at least one delegate was described by William Duer of New York. Duer wrote that Gates seated himself before the delegates "in a very easy, cavalier posture in an elbow chair" and began to list his complaints. As he droned on and on, Duer became disgusted, writing:

"It is impossible . . . to give . . . an idea of the unhappy figure which G.G. made . . . His manner was ungraciously and totally devoid of all dignity, his delivery incoherent and interrupted with frequent chasms in which he was peering over his scattered notes, and the tenor of his discourse a compound of vanity, folly, and rudeness . . . notwithstanding his conduct has been such as to have eradicated from my mind every sentiment of respect and esteem for him, I felt for him as a man and for the honor of human nature wished him to withdraw before he had plunged himself into utter contempt . . ."

Yet this was the man to whom the Congress turned in those dark days when shock at the fall of Ticonderoga and hysteria over Burgoyne's threat swept the nation. Congress voted to give Gates supreme command in the North, with almost dictatorial powers rivaling those of Washington himself. The appointment was made on August 4, but Gates, characteristically, exhibited no passion to speed to the front to save his embattled country. He took so much time on the road between Philadelphia and Albany that it was not until August 19 that he finally relieved Schuyler of command.

By this time, Schuyler, though he was never to get any credit for it, had made many of the moves that were to turn the tide. By this time, too, the Jane McCrea legend had begun to spread and to arouse the countryside. Gates saw its propaganda value; and with his canny schemer's instinct, he taunted Burgoyne for having countenanced such inhuman savagery.

On September 2 he wrote Burgoyne, marveling "that the famous Lieutenant General Burgoyne, in whom the fine Gentleman is united with the Soldier and the Scholar, should hire the savages of America to scalp Europeans and the descendants of Europeans, nay more, that he should pay a price for each scalp so barbarously taken, is more than will be believed in Europe, until authenticated facts shall, in every Gazette, convince mankind of the truth of the horrid fate."

Gates, describing the tragedy of Jane McCrea, making her beautiful, virtuous, dressed in her bridal gown, wrote:

"The miserable fate of Miss McCrea was particularly aggravated by her being dressed to receive her promised husband, but met her murderer employed by you. Upwards of one hundred men, women and children have perished by the hands of the ruffians to whom it is asserted you have paid the price of blood."

Gates showed this letter to Major General Benjamin Lincoln

and the ever-present James Wilkinson, before he dispatched it. Both thought that it went too far since Burgoyne, whatever his faults, had not paid bounties for the scalps of the innocent but, on the contrary, had tried to restrain and control his Indians. But Gates knew a propaganda opportunity when he saw it, and he told them both: "By God! I don't believe either of you can mend it," meaning "better it"—and he sent off the letter to Burgoyne as he had written it.

Two days later, Gates wrote to Governor Jonathan Trumbull of Connecticut: "I gave him [Burgoyne] a Tickler upon Scalping." Gates was proud of his handiwork, and he had a right to be. The courtly, gentlemanly Schuyler would never have written such a letter; but Gates, the intriguer, could and did—and, if one judges by the results, he was justified. Burgoyne wore himself out protesting; it did not matter. He was saddled with the tragic legend of Jane McCrea. Her story was told and retold, as Gates had threatened, in "every Gazette" in the land. Its effect was enormous. New Englanders became convinced that, if such a fate could happen to Jane McCrea—a Tory, the fiancée of a Tory officer—their own wives and children could expect no mercy, but even worse and unimaginable horrors. And so they came swarming from their farms and homesteads, guns in hand, an angry, buzzing swarm intent on giving Gentleman Johnny Burgoyne his comeuppance.

CHAPTER EIGHT

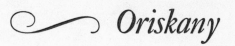 *Oriskany*

BURGOYNE had barely reached the Hudson and suffered the disgrace of the scalping of Jane McCrea when disasters began to strike him, one after another, a series of overwhelming triphammer blows. The first involved one of those supporting, invading arms on which he had counted to help him reach Albany. This was the expedition from the west, led by Lieutenant Colonel Barry St. Leger.

St. Leger was another of those gay, dashing blades so characteristic of the British officer class of the time. He was a fighting Irishman, forty years old, who had spent half of his life in the service. He had fought in the French and Indian War at Louisburg and Quebec, and he was rated a first-class soldier. Like many of his breed, he was overfond of the bottle and of gaming. In 1776 he had founded one of England's horserace classics, the St. Leger, since run annually at Doncaster. Now, a year later, he plunged into the western New York wilderness, his goal a drive down the Mohawk Valley to Albany.

St. Leger's force was a colorful mixture of all the elements that had been brought together by Great Britain in her effort to subdue the rebellious colonists. St. Leger had some 200 British redcoats, a regiment of Tories and a company of Tory rangers, some 100 Hanau jägers, 40 artillerists to handle his cannon, Canadian boatmen and axmen—and, added to all these, a swarm of some 800 to 1000 Indians. In all, he had a force composed of some 875 whites and, with the Indians, a little army of close to 1800 men, a formidable array for that time and place.

The Tories and Indians who joined St. Leger were impelled to do so through old, hard-forged ties. Their loyalties traced back to the influence of one remarkable man who had kept the tribes of the Iroquois, or the Six Nations, loyal to England throughout the century's earlier wars with France. This patriarch was Sir William Johnson, who had been the British Superintendent of Indian Affairs. Johnson had built a baronial mansion on the site of what is now Johnstown, New York. It was like a medieval castle transplanted into the wilderness, manned by a detail of armed guards; from this base of power, Johnson had made his influence felt far and wide.

In cementing his ties with the Six Nations, old Sir William, after the death of his first wife, had honored the daughters of two Indian chiefs by making them his mistresses. The first of these, Caroline, was the daughter of Hendrick, the famous Mohawk leader; the second, whom Johnson reportedly married in an Indian ceremony, was Molly, the shrewd and intelligent sister of a remarkable Indian—Thayendanegea, also known as Joseph Brant, the great war chief of the Mohawks.

Brant had had a fantastic career. He had been educated in English at a school in Connecticut run by Dr. Eleazar Wheelock, who later founded Dartmouth College. With Sir William Johnson's prestige behind him, Brant had visited England, where the young, handsome, and educated Indian from the American wilds had been a novelty and a sensation. He had been entertained by the famous diarist James Boswell and had had his portrait painted by Romney, one of England's foremost artists. Despite all this, Joseph Brant had remained basically an Indian, loyal to his own tribe, and he had now joined with St. Leger to make ruthless war on the settlers of northwestern New York State.

Sir William Johnson had died on the eve of the Revolution, but his heirs carried on. His nephew, Colonel Guy Johnson, became Superintendent of Indian Affairs, and his son, Sir John Johnson, ruled the baronial roost at Johnstown. Allied with them was the powerful Butler family, led by Colonel John and his son, Walter, both of whom had joined Carleton in Canada early in the war. The Butlers, especially Walter, led their Tory followers in such savage forays against their former neighbors that they became more hated and detested than the Indians.

The area for which the Johnsons, the Butlers, Brant—and now St. Leger—were contending was a huge one. It was known as Tryon County, and it stretched all the way from what is now the city of Schenectady to Lake Ontario. The Mohawk River coursed through the region all the way to the Hudson above Albany, creating a beautiful and fertile valley, but one that was sparsely settled. No more than 5000 persons lived in this whole vast region, and they were of mixed nationalities and loyalties—Germans, Dutch, Irish, Scottish Highlanders, and Scotch-Irish. The Germans and many of the Dutch tended to favor the British; the Highlanders were loyal to the King. The entire section was considered a loyalist stronghold, with more Tories than any other county in the northern states.

Yet the Tories had been routed and forced to flee to Canada. This feat had been accomplished by Nicholas Herkimer, a brigadier general of New York militia. Herkimer was fifty, a rugged square-built farmer of German descent, with black hair and snapping dark eyes. He owned large tracts of land in the area around Danube, near what is now Little Falls, where he had built a strong brick mansion that was the talk of the countryside —and a place of refuge in time of trouble.

In 1776, on Schuyler's orders, Herkimer had raised a force of 3000 New York militiamen and led them in an attack on Johnson Hall. Sir John Johnson had been captured and had been given his release after solemnly pledging, on his word of honor, not to engage in hostilities against the Americans for the duration of the war. Shortly afterwards, Sir John had demonstrated that his word of honor wasn't worth very much. Gathering a number of his tenants and other Tories around him, he fled to Montreal, where he organized a two-battalion regiment, the Royal Greens. Commissioned a colonel, he was now returning to do what he had sworn he would never do, making war on the patriots in Tryon County.

With such allies, St. Leger started from Montreal on June 23 and traveled up the St. Lawrence River into Lake Ontario. On July 25—just four days before Burgoyne reached the Hudson at Fort Edward—he was at Oswego, ready to start his drive eastward. A small creek, named like the one at Skenesborough, Wood Creek, flows into Lake Ontario. St. Leger's route lay up this creek, then over a short land portage to the headwaters of the Mohawk. At this strategic point, where an invader from the west would emerge from the woods and try to make use of the broad river pathway, stood an old fort, a relic of the French and Indian War. It was named Fort Stanwix and was located on the site of what is now Rome, New York.

St. Leger had a small artillery train consisting of two six-pounder cannon, two three-pounders, and four small 4.4-inch mortars. With these guns, St. Leger expected to have no trouble blowing the old fort apart. He had been informed that the defenses were in ruins and that the garrison numbered only sixty men. His information accurately reflected the situation as it had existed a few months previously. What St. Leger didn't know, however, was that Schuyler, in spite of all his difficulties, had kept a keen, strategic eye on the danger from the west. In April he had thrown heavy reinforcements into Stanwix, which had been renamed Fort Schuyler in his honor.

Colonel Peter Gansevoort of Albany, with his 3rd New York Continentals, 550 strong, took over the fort. Gansevoort and his active second in command, Lieutenant Colonel Marinus Willett—another of those "bold enterprising" men, as he was called, whom the Revolution seemed to produce in such numbers—had driven their garrison at a furious pace in the few months' grace that they had had. They had repaired the decrepit bastions; had cleared and deepened the surrounding ditch; had combed the smooth slope between bastions and ditch to give their men a clear field of fire. They were ready to fight.

On August 2, at the eleventh hour, they received more help. Some 200 Massachusetts troops, bringing with them stores and ammunition, came in bateaux up the Mohawk. St. Leger heard about this second reinforcement, though he still didn't know of the first; and he dispatched Brant with 200 Indians and some regulars to try to cut the relief column off. Brant was just too late. The Massachusetts soldiers, with their convoy of supplies, just skinned past the raiding Indians and made the fort.

St. Leger's entire force emerged from the woods on August 3. The British leader paraded his men around the fort, apparently hoping to scare the garrison into surrender. However, the sight of nearly 1000 painted, prancing, howling Indians had an effect the very opposite of that intended. The war whoops of the savages reminded the defenders of what fate probably awaited them if they surrendered, what cruelties would be practiced on the entire countryside. They became more determined than ever to resist; and when St. Leger sent them a pompous and bombastic demand for surrender, they treated it with contempt, not even deigning to answer it.

The invading army now ringed the fort, and the Indians crept close, firing at every head that showed itself above the parapets. As one soldier wrote on August 4: "A continual firing of small arms was this day kept up by the enemy's Indians, who advanced within gunshot of the fort, in small parties under the cover of bushes, weeds and potatoes in the garden . . . The firing ended with the close of the day, we having one man killed and six wounded." The following day, another man "was shot dead on the northeast bastion," and new barracks that had been built about 100 yards outside the fort were set on fire.

While this skirmishing was going on, the defenders kept throwing up sandbags to strengthen the defenses and increase their height. St. Leger saw that he could never reduce the fort unless he brought up his artillery, and so he sent back a large detachment of his men to hack a road sixteen miles long through the dense forests. He was so occupied when, on August 5, he learned that a relief force was marching toward the fort.

Nicholas Herkimer was on the move. He had issued a call for militia to rally around him on July 30 at Fort Dayton, about thirty miles below Stanwix, taking with him a wagon train containing ammunition and supplies. As he neared the fort, Herkimer sent ahead three messengers telling the defenders of his approach. Herkimer asked Gansevoort to acknowledge receipt of the message by firing three guns and then to launch an attack on the British lines from the fort while Herkimer slashed at them from the outside.

The circle of Indians around the fort was so tight that the messengers could not get through at once, and so no guns were fired. Worried, Herkimer halted his force and called a council of war. He wanted to wait until the fort replied to his message, but his officers were determined to plunge ahead. The council developed into an angry, bitter session. One of Herkimer's brothers was a Tory officer serving under St. Leger, and some of Herkimer's followers now implied that their general was a coward or, perhaps, even a Tory at heart. This was too much for the courageous and patriotic Herkimer. He gave the order to advance and led them all, an unmistakable figure on a large white horse.

St. Leger was ready. Six miles from Stanwix, near Oriskany Village, the wilderness road Herkimer was following dipped down into a wide ravine, flanked on either side by steep wooded hills. A small stream ran through the bottom of the ravine, bridged by a rough span of loosely laid logs. Herkimer's advancing column had to narrow its line of march and pass slowly through this bottleneck. The place was ideal for an ambush.

Hoping to wipe out Herkimer's entire force, St. Leger set the trap with care. He posted a part of Johnson's Royal Greens, a detachment of Butler's Rangers, and his entire force of Indians in the surrounding woods. Joseph Brant had command. Herkimer's Oneida Indians should have discovered so large a force, but they didn't. Unsuspecting, Herkimer on his white horse led his column down into the ravine, across the log bridge, and up the opposite slope. The creaking oxcarts of his supply train groaned down behind him to the bridge. His whole force except for a small rear guard was in the trap when the woods on every side suddenly burst into a blaze of rifle and musket fire, accompanied by the hair-raising war whoops of the Indians.

Herkimer's rear guard promptly fled, pursued by the Indians. Herkimer himself was wounded in one leg, his horse shot from under him. His men were completely encircled. No situation could have been more desperate.

Coolly, despite his wound, Herkimer rallied his men. His saddle was brought and propped against a tree in the center of his embattled force. Seating himself upon it, smoking his pipe with apparent unconcern, Herkimer ordered his men to take cover, wilderness fashion, behind stumps and trees and to fire outward at the enemy that ringed them on every side.

For three quarters of an hour the bloody conflict raged back and forth in that dark woodland trap. Much of it was hand-to-hand work. As soon as an American fired, an Indian would dash upon him with upraised tomahawk before he could load his gun again. The Tories jabbed with the bayonet and were met with clubbed muskets. At the peak of the battle, a sudden summer storm came up, and the downpour drenched the powder in the flintlock guns, making firing impossible. For an hour there was a pause in the fighting. Then the sun came out, and the battle was resumed—but now with a difference. Herkimer had used the lull to reorganize his forces. He now stationed his men in pairs behind every stump and tree; and so, when one fired and an Indian rushed forward to brain him, the Indian himself fell victim to the fire of the second.

This kind of warfare was not to the Indians' liking. This was not the merry scalping party they had envisioned. Their fire slackened; they began to waver. At this point, a second detachment of the Royal Greens tried to save the day. Their major made them turn their green jackets inside out, hoping to make Herkimer's men believe they were Americans sallying from the fort. The ruse was discovered in time, however. Herkimer's troops launched a fierce attack, and a deadly combat followed.

This was too much for the Indians. "Oonah! Oonah!" they cried, their signal for retreat. Like shadows, they faded away into the woods; and the Tories, abandoned, had no choice but to follow.

Herkimer's force had not been wiped out, but it had been so badly mauled that it could not accomplish its mission, the relief of Stanwix. It had to retreat.

There was no accurate count of losses at this bloody Battle of Oriskany. The best estimate was that between 150 and 200 of Herkimer's 800 men had been killed; another fifty, including the general who was soon to die from his injury and crude surgery, had been wounded and had to be carried from the field on litters. Tory and Indian losses were estimated at about 150 men.

Herkimer's gallant fight had also made possible a second action of no small psychological significance. When firing broke out in the Oriskany trap, the general's long-delayed messengers managed to slip into Stanwix, and the fort's defenders decided to launch a surprise attack of their own. Marinus Willett in a rousing speech called for volunteers, and an attacking force of 250 men was swiftly organized.

As soon as the shower ended that had forced a pause in the fighting at Oriskany, fiery Willett launched his sortie directly at Sir John Johnson's headquarters in St. Leger's camp. He drove his thrust home with such speed and force that the headquarters guard was quickly scattered, and Sir John had to flee without pausing even to don his coat. Willett's victorious raiders loaded twenty-one wagons with the spoils of victory—clothing, blankets, stores, camp equipage, five British standards, Sir John's baggage and all his official papers, and the property and correspondence of other officers. It was a heady triumph, accomplished without the loss of a single man.

Despite this, the situation in the beleaguered fort was if anything more hopeless than before. Herkimer had been turned back, and no other relief was in sight. St. Leger drew his siege lines ever tighter. He sent an officer into the fort under a flag of truce with another demand for surrender. If the fort's defenders did not yield at once, he warned, he could not guarantee their safety; they must expect massacre at the hands of the Indians. Marinus Willett, who emerged as the real hero of the resistance, boiled with anger as he listened and replied with heat and scorn. He told St. Leger's emissary:

"I consider the message you have brought a degrading one for a British officer to send, and by no means reputable for a British officer to carry. For my own part, I declare, before I would consent to deliver this garrison to such a murdering set as your army, by your own account, consists of, I would suffer my body to be filled with splinters and set on fire, as you know has at times been practiced by such hordes of women-and-children killers as belong to your army."

Bold, defiant words. Heroic words. But they did not change the situation. Fort Stanwix was still in desperate plight, with little prospect of relief coming soon enough. It was at this moment that Philip Schuyler showed his caliber.

The American commander in chief in the North, not yet relieved by Gates, called a council of war in his camp at Stillwater. Not far away was Burgoyne's menacing, powerful army. To meet it Schuyler had only the most pitiful forces. Yet he did not hesitate for a moment. He was determined to save Fort Stanwix.

His officers, almost to a man, were opposed to the attempt. How could he even think of weakening his already powerless army in the face of Burgoyne's threat? Some even muttered to Schuyler's face that such a diversion of his forces indicated he must be a traitor at heart. In his anger, Schuyler bit the stem of his clay pipe in half. Throwing away the pieces, he stared down his officers in the haughty manner of the insulted patrician and told them coldly: "Gentlemen, I shall take the responsibility upon myself. Fort Stanwix and the Mohawk Valley shall be saved! Where is the brigadier who will command the relief? I shall beat up for volunteers tomorrow."

These ringing words struck a responsive chord in at least one of his high-ranking officers. Impetuous as ever, Benedict Arnold sprang forward. He was furious at the slurs cast at Schuyler. It was a strange affinity, this relationship of Arnold and Schuyler: Arnold, the flawed hero, devoured by inner cankers of ambition and lust for recognition, power, money; Schuyler, the landed gentleman, courtly in his ways, lacking the common touch, the soul of honor. What drew the two together, doubtless, was a mutual, deep-seated dedication to the patriot cause and the recognition by each of this dedication in the other, the respect of each for the other's abilities. The result was that Arnold became a thorough-going partisan of the much-maligned Schuyler.

Volunteers flocked to Arnold as they always did, for he inspired more faith in his fighting ability than any other American general at this period. With 950 men, a force only a little larger than the one headed by Herkimer that had been cut up at Oriskany, Arnold set out to relieve Fort Stanwix. He moved with his usual swiftness and by August 23 he was not far from the fort. Here he demonstrated that he was more than a headlong, impetuous fighter; he could also be as wily as a fox.

Knowing that St. Leger's army still outnumbered him almost two to one, Arnold decided upon a ruse. The Americans had arrested a half-demented Tory, Hon Yost Schuyler, whose father was a cousin of General Schuyler and whose mother was Herkimer's sister, for trying to recruit men for the British cause. Hon Yost had been sentenced to death; but Arnold, learning of this, stayed the sentence and offered Hon Yost a choice.

Arnold knew that the Indians had a great, superstitious respect for the mentally deranged whom the Great Father for mysterious reasons of his own had affected. They credited such afflicted persons with prophetic vision. What would happen, Arnold wondered, if Hon Yost were to burst suddenly into the British camp with the word that he had just escaped from the clutches of an overwhelming American army? Hon Yost, offered the choice of acting out this role or being executed, made the obvious decision.

He took off his coat, and the Americans fired a number of

bullet holes through it to lend credence to his story. Then Hon Yost, accompanied by an Oneida Indian, set out for St. Leger's camp. He rushed in, to all appearance a terrified and babbling figure. An American host, led by the terrible Arnold, was almost upon them, he cried; he himself had just managed to escape with his life—and he exhibited his bullet-riddled jacket as proof. The Oneida Indian confirmed his story. He informed his red brothers that Arnold was about to fall upon them at the head of 3000 men.

The Indians, with their respect for the insane, never doubted Hon Yost's fabrication. Indians and British alike feared Arnold more than any other American officer. The idea that he was about to attack them with 3000 men threw the Indians into panic. Nothing that St. Leger or Sir John Johnson could do had any effect. The Indians rioted. They seized the officers' supplies of liquor and some of their clothing. They became, St. Leger wrote, "more formidable than the enemy!"

Hon Yost, all by himself, had routed an army. Such was the terror his tale inspired that Indians, British, and Tories all fled into the woods, leaving their artillery, ammunition and supplies behind them. And Benedict Arnold marched into Fort Stanwix without firing a shot.

It was a weird and great victory. One of those all-conquering, invading arms that Burgoyne had expected to link up with him at Albany had been lopped off and scattered in headlong flight. No matter how desperate his need, he would get no help from the west.

CHAPTER NINE

 *Bennington*

BACK ON THE HUDSON, storm clouds gathered about the head of Gentleman Johnny. He felt no need to worry at this time, in early August, about St. Leger's thrust from the west. Surely that would go well. But he knew that he could expect no help from New York.

The incredible blundering and cross-purposes that had marked the planning of the campaign from the moment Lord George Germain decided he could not keep his horses waiting now bore its inevitable, bitter fruit. In New York Sir William Howe determined, as he had indicated, to leave Burgoyne to his own devices and go off on his own campaign against Philadelphia.

The decision was not popular with his own officers. Sir Henry Clinton, Howe's second in command, who was to be left behind to hold New York, never had believed that Burgoyne could reach Albany on his own; and he argued long and bitterly with Howe, trying to make him see the obvious—the necessity for a drive up the Hudson to aid Burgoyne and crush the Americans between two powerful armies. But Howe refused to see.

On July 17 he wrote Burgoyne a cheerful, good-old-chap letter, informing Gentleman Johnny that he was off to Philadelphia. Howe put it this way: "My intention is for Pennsylvania, where I expect to meet Washington, but if he goes northward, contrary to my expectations, and you can keep him at bay, be assured I will soon be after him to relieve you . . . Success be ever with you."

This letter reached Burgoyne on August 3 at Fort Edward; and by that time, though Burgoyne could not know it, there was no chance that Howe would ever come chasing north after Washington no matter what Washington did. For Howe, instead of campaigning on land, a strategy that would have kept contact with Washington's opposing army, had embarked his troops in the ships of the British fleet, sailing all the way to Chesapeake Bay to attack Philadelphia from the south. By August 3 he was at sea off the Delaware capes and out of touch with everything.

Gentleman Johnny, whose spirits went up and down like a yo-yo, appears not to have worried very much at the moment about what Howe was doing. Having survived the brutal trials of the Skenesborough-Fort Edward march, having reached the Hudson, Burgoyne and his army "considered their toils to be nearly at an end; Albany to be within their grasp, and the adjacent provinces certainly reduced." So optimistic was Gentleman Johnny that he filed Howe's letter in his pocket, telling no one on his staff about it; and on August 6, in reply to Howe, he predicted with confidence that he would be in Albany by August 23.

There were, of course, a few difficulties to be dealt with in the meantime. As a Hessian officer with Burgoyne's army wrote: "Though our troops had toiled without intermission for three whole weeks, there was in camp no greater stock of provisions than sufficed for four days consumption; and to move forward with a supply so slender into a desert country appeared to a leader of the old school little better than insanity." The officer explained that the countryside "heaven knows was sterile enough," but it had been swept so clean as a result of Schuyler's "scorched earth" policy that "every particle of grain, as well as morsel of grass" had been burned or removed.

A second problem also called for solution. Burgoyne never had been able to obtain half the horses that he needed. Baron von Riedesel's dragoons were horseless. They had had to trudge along on foot, encumbered by uniforms and equipment that horses, not men, had been intended to bear. They wore stiff leather breeches, high cocked hats, great clumsy boots and spurs that constantly caught in roots and underbrush as they struggled along. Their long sabers clanked against rocks and became entangled in wilderness vines; and their heavy carbines, which horses could have borne like feathers, became intolerable burdens for men.

Von Riedesel wanted horses, and, before the army left Skenesborough, he had suggested to Burgoyne a raid into Vermont to get them. Burgoyne had approved the plan, and now at Fort Edward he decided to put it into effect. He recognized that there might be difficulties, for as he later said, "the New Hampshire Grants [as Vermont was then called] . . . now abounds in the most active and rebellious race on the continent, and hangs like a gathering storm on my left."

It was typical of Burgoyne, the optimist, the gambler, that he preferred at the time to ignore the dangers of this "gathering storm" and listen to the siren voice of the man who always told him what he wanted to hear—Philip Skene. Skene, who was supposed to know the countryside, assured Burgoyne that the Vermont hills held not just rambunctious rebels, but thousands of eager Tories who would flock to his banner once they saw the British colors. Accepting the advice of this resident expert, Burgoyne sent Skene along with the expedition so that he could "distinguish good subjects from bad."

The Americans in the meantime had not been idle. They had recognized that Burgoyne might do exactly what he was now planning to do, and they had taken steps to counter such a move. Again these steps depended in large measure on the broad strategic vision of Philip Schuyler. Desperately pressed as he was, with his army little more than a rabble after the fall of Ticonderoga and St. Clair's long retreat, Schuyler nevertheless refused to try to strengthen his forces at the expense of New

Hampshire and Vermont. In a letter written to Seth Warner on July 16, in the darkest of dark days, Schuyler said he had been told New Hampshire militia were coming to join him. Then, in a largeness of spirit that has to excite admiration, he added: "It is not my intention, much as I am in want of troops, that they should come hither, as it would expose the country in that quarter to the depredations of the enemy." Schuyler, almost destitute of funds to maintain his own army, scraped together $4000 which he sent along to Warner with an accompanying order to the New Hampshire militia to place themselves under Warner's command and defend their own countryside.

Burgoyne was aware that Warner, who had fought so well at Hubbardton, was gathering forces in the Vermont hills; but he did not know that his foraging expedition would encounter a commander even more to be dreaded—John Stark.

Stark was without doubt one of the ablest and most valiant fighters in the American army. He was also a man whose military career, fortunately as it turned out, had been cut short, sacrificed to petty politics in the Continental Congress. Stark, a captain in Roger's Rangers in the French and Indian War and a noted Indian fighter, looked himself much like an Indian —tall, straight, sinewy, with a long nose, high cheekbones, piercing blue eyes, and thin determined lips. Those clamped-down lips gave the clue to his stubborn character. In New England, noted for cantankerous characters, John Stark stood out as one of the most cantankerous.

He had joined the army at the very outbreak of the Revolution. He had commanded the left wing of the patriot forces at the Battle of Bunker Hill and had done deadly execution against the charging British ranks. He had taken part in the invasion of Canada. He had crossed the ice-choked Delaware with Washington in the surprise attack at Trenton; he had fought valiantly at Princeton. On every field on which he had been engaged he had distinguished himself; but when it came time for promotion, the politicians in Congress had passed him over, jumping junior officers of far lesser merit over his head. Not even Congress could do this to the Cantankerous Man. Proud, irascible, John

Stark said, in effect, to the devil with Congress and all its works. He threw up his commission and returned to his New Hampshire hills, vowing never again to serve in the Continental Army or to submit to any orders from a Continental Army officer. Nor did he.

By divorcing himself in this fashion from the mainstream of the war, John Stark became the right man at the right spot at the right time when Burgoyne's invading forces threatened Vermont and New Hampshire. Stark was so well known and so admired by his New England neighbors that there was never any question who should command the militia forces they now raised. Speaker John Langdon of the New Hampshire General Court, or legislature, expressed the prevailing sentiment on July 18 when he said: "We can raise a brigade, and our friend John Stark may be safely entrusted with the command, and we will check Burgoyne."

Stark, sulking on his farm along the Merrimack River, agreed to return to the war on just one condition: his was to be a totally independent command, subject to no one's orders but his own. This was agreed to, and the magic of Stark's name helped to arouse the countryside. One New Hampshire historian later described the reaction in the town of Concord in these words:

"As soon as it was decided to raise volunteer companies and place them under the command of Gen. Stark, Col. Hutchins (delegate from Concord) mounted his horse, and traveling all night with all possible haste, reached Concord on Sabbath afternoon, before the close of public service. Dismounting at the meeting-house door, he walked up the aisle of the church while Mr. Walker was preaching. Mr. Walker paused in his sermon, and said: 'Col. Hutchins, are you the bearer of any message?' 'Yes,' replied the Colonel: 'Gen. Burgoyne, with his army, is on his march to Albany. Gen. Stark has offered to take command of the New Hampshire men; and, if we all turn out, we can cut off Burgoyne's march.' Whereupon Rev. Mr. Walker said: 'My hearers, those of you who are willing to go, better leave at once.' At which word all the men in the meeting-house rose and went out. Many immediately enlisted. The whole night was spent in preparation, and a company was ready to march the next day."

The response was so enthusiastic that in just six days 1492 officers and men enlisted to serve under Stark. Stark at once took the field, sending 700 men to join Warner at Manchester and following himself with another 300 on August 9. When he arrived, he found himself confronted with a situation that, except for his own stubborn independence, would have ruined everything.

After the fall of Ticonderoga, Washington, recognizing that Schuyler was heartily disliked in New England, had sent Major General Benjamin Lincoln north to bolster morale. Lincoln, who was so obese that any horse would have been justified in shuddering at the prospect of carrying him, thus became the senior officer in the field, and he was preparing to march the newly raised New Hampshire militia to join Schuyler at Stillwater. Schuyler himself, faced with the threat to Fort Stanwix from the west and desperately needing men, had reversed his earlier July decision and ordered the move. When Stark arrived at Manchester, he found his troops all packed up and ready to march. He quickly put a stop to that. He told Lincoln, as the latter reported, that he felt himself "adequate to command his own men"; he would not go to Stillwater on the orders of Schuyler or anyone except the General Court of New Hampshire. With that, Stark marched off to Bennington and destiny.

Lincoln's report on all this caused great anger in Congress over Stark's "insubordination." Schuyler, however, as soon as he heard the first rumors of Burgoyne's excursion into Vermont, saw the wisdom of Stark's move, went back to his original July order instructing New Hampshire men to fight on their own grounds, and even offered to send Stark another 500 troops. Before this could be done, however, Stark had proved his worth in battle and had won a victory that could not have been achieved if he had not, by his "insubordination," kept his troops in the right spot to fight.

A veteran of the Battle of Bennington later gave this description of Stark's little army:

"To a man, they wore small-clothes, coming down and fastening just below the knee, and long stockings with cowhide shoes ornamented by large buckles, while not a pair of boots graced the company. The coats and waistcoats were loose and of huge dimensions, with colors as various as the barks of oaks, sumach and other trees of our hills and swamps could make them, and their shirts were all made of flax and, like every other part of the dress, were homespun. On their heads was worn a large round-top and broad-brimmed hat. Their arms were as various as their costume. Here an old soldier carried a heavy Queen's Arm, with which he had done service at the conquest of Canada twenty years previous, while by his side walked a stripling boy, with a Spanish fusee not half its weight or calibre, which his grandfather may have taken at the Havana, while not a few had old French pieces that dated back to the reduction of Louisburg. Instead of the cartridge box, a large powder horn was slung under the arm, and occasionally a bayonet might be seen bristling in the ranks. Some of the swords of the officers had been made by our Province blacksmiths, perhaps from some farming utensil; they looked serviceable, but heavy and uncouth."

Pitted against these rustic warriors was a foraging party of about 650 troops led by Lieutenant Colonel Friedrich Baum, a German who could not "utter one word of English" and who, as a consequence, seemed the worst possible choice to head such an expedition. Baum's force consisted of 170 of his own jack-booted dragoons, 100 German grenadiers and light infantry, some 300 Tories, Canadians, and Indians, 50 British marksmen, and a small artillery contingent to handle two field-pieces.

Burgoyne spelled out the purposes of the foray. Baum was "to try the affections of the people, to disconcert the councils of the enemy." He was to obtain mounts for Von Riedesel's dragoons and "to obtain large supplies of cattle, horses and carriages." Burgoyne envisioned obtaining 1300 horses in addition to those needed for the dragoons, and these were to be "tied together by strings of ten each, in order that one man may lead ten horses." Baum was authorized to hold "the most respectable people" as hostages until he got the horses and supplies he needed, and he was also to make prisoners of "all persons acting in committees, or any officers under the direction of Congress, whether civil or military."

This was a large order for a force of only 650 men. It was made even larger on the eve of Baum's departure. Von Riedesel's original proposal had called only for a limited raid into nearby districts close to the main army; but Burgoyne heard that the Americans were amassing a large depot of stores and ammunition at Bennington, Vermont—and so he directed Baum to march there, pressing much farther into a hostile countryside than had been originally contemplated. Von Riedesel expressed "fear and astonishment" when he learned of this change of plan, but obstinate Burgoyne refused to be swayed by his protests.

On August 11 Baum marched. From the outset he had trouble with his Indians. They ranged ahead of his main body, looting, killing, destroying property. They killed cows for the sake of their cowbells instead of rounding them up to provide meat for the army; they drove off horses instead of capturing them so that Baum could tie them up in those strings of ten. Such depredations only helped, of course, to arouse the countryside against the invaders.

Even without an Indian contingent that did more harm than good, Baum's task would have been difficult enough. His jackbooted, heavily accoutered dragoons could not move swiftly through the wild country into which they plunged. A Hessian officer described it this way: "About twenty miles to the eastward of the Hudson lies the obscure village of Bennington, a cluster of poor cottages situated in a wild country between the forks of the Hosac . . . One prodigious forest, bottomed in swamps and morasses, covered the whole face of the country, through which no body of men, unless accustomed to such expeditions, could hope to make their way, at all events with celerity."

The slow, crawling approach of Baum's raiders gave Stark time to make his plans and rally forces to meet them. He sent out a scouting party of 200 men to harass Baum. These militiamen fired one volley at the advancing enemy and then decamped, burning a bridge behind them to insure their escape and delay Baum. After this almost bloodless skirmish, Baum, using the head of a barrel for a desk, dashed off this note to Burgoyne:

"By five prisoners taken here, they agree that fifteen hundred to eighteen hundred men are in Bennington, but are supposed to leave it on our approach. I will proceed so far today as to fall on the enemy tomorrow early and make such dispositions as I think necessary from the intelligence I may receive. People are flocking in hourly but want to be armed. The savages cannot be controlled; they ruin and take everything they please."

This information that he had a large-sized and hostile force in his front, instead of the few weak militia units he had expected, should have given Baum cause for thought, but it did not. He plunged ahead, and about four miles west of Bennington, late in the afternoon of August 14, he sighted Stark's main force. The Walloomsac River ran between the two hostile armies. Stark, in his report on the battle, later described what happened next: "I drew up my little army in order of battle, but when the enemy hove in sight, they halted on a very advantageous hill or piece of ground. I sent out small parties in their front to skirmish with them, which scheme had a good effect. They killed or wounded thirty of the enemy without any loss on our side, but the ground that I was upon did [not] suit for a general action. I marched back one mile and incamped. Called a counsel, and it was agreed we should send two detachments in their rear, while others attacked them in front."

A torrential rain now descended upon the countryside, making action impossible. The storm, accompanied by howling winds, lasted all day on August 15, and both sides, huddled in their camps, waited for the weather to clear, and called up reinforcements. Additional Tories joined Baum, bringing his force up to about 800 men. Stark did better; he was joined by another 400 Vermont militiamen and some Stockbridge Indians.

He now had about 2000 men under his command, and he sent out word to Seth Warner's regiment, camped at Manchester, to march to join him.

Baum, by now realizing that he faced a gathering host, was having some worrisome thoughts. He dispatched another letter to Burgoyne, telling him of his plight and asking for reinforcements. Roused from bed to read the message, Burgoyne summoned Von Riedesel and ordered him to dispatch Lieutenant Colonel Heinrich C. von Breymann with 550 men and two six-pounder cannon to the relief of Baum. Again, in a situation that called for speed, Burgoyne relied on the heavily burdened, slow-moving Germans. Von Breymann marched on the morning of August 15, plodding forward in accepted military style, pausing frequently to dress the ranks. He was also slowed down by the torrent that was postponing action at Bennington. The wilderness tracks he followed were turned into a morass of mud, his cannons became mired and had to be pried from the sucking goo; and, between the weather and the constant dressing of ranks in proper military form, Von Breymann, as he later wrote, "could scarcely make one-half an English mile an hour."

Some of the Americans facing Baum were getting impatient at the delay. Among the new militia forces that had joined Stark was a contingent from Pittsfield, Massachusetts, led by a fighting parson, Thomas Allen. Allen charged into Stark's cabin and demanded permission to attack the enemy. "Would you go out on this dark and rainy night?" Stark asked. He then told the fire-eating parson, "Go back to your people, and tell them to get some rest if they can, and if the Lord gives us some sunshine, and I do not give you fighting enough, I will never ask you to come out again."

The Lord co-operated. On August 16 the storm ended, the skies cleared, the sun came out—and the battle was on.

The heart of Baum's position was a steep, 300-foot hill, later named Hessian Hill, that overlooked the Walloomsac River separating the two little armies. Baum stationed his 170 dragoons, some 20 of the British marksmen, and some Indians on the crest of the hill. Trees had been felled to make breastworks, and one of Baum's three-pounder cannon was placed there. Directly in front of the hill was a patch of swampy ground leading to Little White Creek. The Walloomsac flowed around to Baum's left and rear, where a bridge spanned the stream. To keep the Americans from crossing the span, Baum had thrown up more breastworks at both ends of the bridge and had placed his second cannon there.

Stark now devised a sweeping, ambitious battle plan designed to bag Baum's entire force. He dispatched Colonel Moses Nichols' regiment of 200 men to circle around to Baum's left and rear beyond the bridge. He ordered Colonel Samuel Herrick with 300 men to make a similar encircling movement to the right and rear. Colonels David Hobart and Thomas Stickney were to come down the Bennington road and strike directly at the bridge. Stark himself would lead the remainder of his forces in a charge up the front of the hill from the marshy land along Little White Creek. By three o'clock in the afternoon, all of Stark's men were in position and ready to strike.

In the British camp there was fatal confusion. Much of it traced back to Philip Skene. So divorced from reality was this expert adviser that he kept telling Colonel Baum that the countryside abounded in Tories over rebels by a margin of five to one. As a result, Baum welcomed every shirt-sleeved, homespun-clad stranger who wandered into his camp displaying a white piece of paper in his cap to indicate allegiance to the true faith. British officers who had fought at Hubbardton could have told him that the rebels were capable of playing just such tricks, and even some of Baum's Hessian officers, without the Hubbardton experience to rely on, found their commander's blind acceptance of all these strangers simply incredible.

The Hessian officer who had described the wilderness countryside in such graphic terms wrote that "during the last day's march our little corps was joined by many of the country people, most of whom demanded and obtained arms, as persons friendly to the royal cause. How Colonel Baum became so completely duped as to place reliance on these men, I know not;

but having listened with complacency to their previous assurances that in Bennington a large majority of the populace were our friends, he was somehow or other persuaded to believe that the armed bands, of whose approach he was warned, were loyalists on their way to make tender of their services to the leader of the king's troops."

Even with the battle about to begin, Baum persisted in his delusion. He ordered his pickets not to fire on the approaching bands, but even to withdraw, giving up their posts to the homespun strangers who thankfully occupied them and crouched, waiting for the signal to fire. It came when Nichols' and Herrick's men shouted and let loose a fusillade at Baum from the rear. The Hessian officer's account continues:

". . . The column in our front no sooner heard the shout than they replied cordially and loudly to it; then, firing a volley with deliberate and murderous aim, rushed furiously towards us. Now then, at length, our leader's dreams of security were dispelled. He found himself attacked in front and flanked by thrice his number . . . whilst the very persons in whom he had trusted, and to whom he had given arms, lost no time in turning them against him. These followers no sooner heard their comrades' cry than they deliberately discharged their muskets among Riedesel's dragoons and, dispersing before any steps could be taken to seize them, escaped, excepting one or two, to their friends."

With Nichols and Herrick, whose forces had joined in one unbroken line, hammering at the British rear, Hobart and Stickney launched their attack on the breastworks guarding the bridge. And Stark, marshaling his men at the foot of the hill, gave the order for the main frontal attack. Local tradition has it that he cried: "See there, men! There they are! We'll beat them before night, or Molly Stark will be a widow."

The breastworks by the river bridge were carried with a rush. The Americans waited until the defenders had fired one volley, then charged before they could reload their guns. The enemy in the breastworks scattered in flight. The Indians, yelling and jingling their stolen cowbells, fled like flitting shadows into the forest, led by their commander, St. Luc de La Corne. Abandoned by their allies, the Hessians on the hill fought with utmost desperation.

The very steepness of the hill below their lines hampered them. They could not depress their cannon enough to do execution, and Stark's men clambered upward, taking cover behind every rock and stump, firing so fast their gun barrels began to burn their hands. As Stark later reported, the battle "lasted 2 hours, the hotest I ever saw in my life. It represented one continued clap of thunder."

Some of the New Hampshire militia crept up the hill to within a dozen yards of the fieldpiece and shot down all the gunners. Beset on all sides, Baum's men began to waver, their fire to slacken; the Americans stormed the top of the hill, bursting upon the defenders from all directions. At this point, according to the Hessian officer, "The solitary tumbril which contained the whole of our spare ammunition became ignited and blew up with a violence that shook the very ground under our feet and caused a momentary cessation in firing, both on our side and that of the enemy."

The stunned pause lasted only for a moment; then the Americans launched their final charge. "For a few seconds the scene that ensued defies the power of language to describe," the Hessian wrote. "The bayonet, the butt of the rifle, the sabre, the pike, were in full play, and men fell, as they rarely fall in modern war, under the direct blows of their enemies."

The situation was hopeless, and Baum called upon his dragoons to drop their guns and charge with heavy sabers. The Americans had few bayonets with which to defend themselves, and some of the dragoons, including the Hessian officer who lived to write about it, hacked their way through and lumbered off into the surrounding woods. In this final charge, Baum was shot in the stomach and mortally wounded, and those of his men who were left on the hilltop threw down their arms and surrendered.

Victorious, some of the Americans rushed after the fugitives who had fled into the woods. Lightfooted as Indians, they tracked down many of the blundering dragoons, whose spurs caught and tripped them up and whose ponderous swords became entangled in the underbrush. As evidence of the bloody work that went on in that gloomy forest, there is the account of an American farmer who wrote a week later: "We do not know how many we have killed. Our scouts daily find them dead in the woods. One of our scouts found, the beginning of this week, twenty-six of the enemy lying dead in the woods."

While this pursuit was spreading out across the countryside, back on the crest of Hessian Hill all was disorder. Stark, to encourage his men, had promised them that the fruits of victory should be theirs, and the joyous militia were now engaged in a happy looting party. With affairs in such a disordered state, disaster now suddenly threatened.

Von Breymann, much too late, was arriving on the field. He encountered his first party of disorganized, shirt-sleeved men about a mile from the battlefield. Philip Skene, who had ridden back to urge him on, was certain that they must be Tories. Who else? Spurring his horse, he galloped up a slope toward the strangers, shouting: "Are you for King George?" He was only 100 yards away when he got his answer—a burst of gunfire that shot his horse right out from under him. If this was not enough to disillusion the ever-optimistic Skene, it certainly convinced Von Breymann. He pressed on, firing at every group of armed rustics he encountered. The Americans fell back— and back. Stark, who had so recently routed Baum's forces on Hessian Hill, now faced rout himself.

But at this crucial moment Seth Warner's men from Manchester came charging on the field. Stark rallied fragments of his own troops around them and took up a position on a wooded hill north of the Bennington road. Von Breymann charged. Warner's men outflanked him and poured in a deadly fire. Head to head, the new battle raged. Von Breymann brought up his two six-pounder cannon and blazed away. Musketry fire made one continuous thunder of sound. On and on it went until Von Breymann's troops began to be exhausted and their powder ran low. They had entered the battle with only forty rounds of ammunition per man, and by sunset it was almost all expended. But the American fire kept up, unbroken and deadly.

Beaten, Von Breymann tried to withdraw. The retreat became a rout. Some Germans threw down their muskets and ran. Others kneeled and cried for mercy. Von Breymann himself was ready to surrender. He had his drums beat out the signal for a parley; but the sound, which would have been recognized on a European battlefield, meant nothing to the Americans. They kept right on shooting.

Von Breymann organized a small rear guard and tried to hold them off. He was wounded in one leg, and there were five bullet holes in his coat. Still he fought on. And by fighting, as night came, he saved the remnants of his force. "Had day lasted an hour longer," Stark wrote later, "we should have taken the whole body of them."

As it was, Bennington was a tremendous victory. Untrained American countrymen, coming to battle with all kinds of ancient weapons, had overwhelmed two bodies of trained, professional soldiers. They had captured four brass fieldpieces, twelve drums, 250 sabers, four ammunition wagons, and several hundred muskets and rifles. They had lost only 30 killed and 40 wounded. They had killed 207 Germans and Tories and captured 700, including 30 officers.

The psychological and strategic effects were enormous. Americans exulted in the victory and came swarming in ever greater numbers to finish off Burgoyne. As for Gentleman Johnny himself, he had been rocked back on his heels. He had lost nearly 1000 men whom he could not hope to replace; he had the wilderness behind him, a gathering host in front. The trap was beginning to close; and he began to pray now, much too late in the game, for the kind of help from Sir William Howe that, in his first glorious flush of overconfidence, he had never thought to need.

CHAPTER TEN

The Gambler Plunges

LICKING his wounds after Bennington, Burgoyne sat for some three weeks on the upper Hudson, trying to decide on his next move and gathering supplies. The way his mind shuttled back and forth between despair and hope—now assailed with forebodings of defeat, now buoyed by visions of final victory—was illustrated in a letter he wrote to Lord George Germain on August 20, 1777.

This revealed, among other things, that Burgoyne was now looking to New York City and hoping for succor from Sir William Howe, who, with his army and Mrs. Loring, was making the long detour up the Chesapeake to attack Philadelphia from the south. "Another most embarrassing circumstance [in addition to the "gathering storm" in Vermont]," Burgoyne wrote, "is the want of communication with Sir William Howe; of the messengers I have sent, I know of two being hanged, and am ignorant whether any of the rest arrived . . . No operation, my Lord, has yet been undertaken in my favour . . ."

The sensible thing would have been to retreat, to fall back to Fort Ticonderoga and wait for another season, reinforcements, and a co-ordinated battle plan. But Burgoyne did not have that stubborn jaw for nothing. He was an obstinate man, and this obstinacy, which in another situation might have been a virtue, now brought him to turn his back on common-sense, strategic withdrawal. He argued that his orders gave him no "latitude," but were "positive," instructing him to "force a junction with Sir William Howe." He recognized that if he plunged deeper into the hostile countryside, he would lose all communication with Canada; it would be impossible to protect his long supply line to the north. Even if he reached Albany, he would have to live off the countryside. Still, because his orders were "positive," he was determined; he would plunge ahead.

Having announced this bold decision, Burgoyne turned around and moaned to Germain about the lack of help from New York—a circumstance of which he had been fully aware before he left Canada and one that had not seemed so important to him then. "When I wrote more confidently," Burgoyne told Germain, "I little foresaw that I was to be left to pursue my way through such a tract of country and hosts of foes, without any co-operation from New-York . . ." Yet he assured Germain, in another switch, "I do not despond."

Germain's reaction was typical. In a note penned September 29 he confided he was "sorry" Burgoyne was "disappointed" about Howe, but added "the more honour for Burgoyne if he does the business without any assistance from New York." A month later on October 31—it seems to have taken that long for the implications of Burgoyne's report to penetrate the slow Germain mind—the minister wrote another memorandum in which he said "what alarms me most is that he [Burgoyne] thinks his orders to go to Albany to force a junction with Sir William Howe are so positive that he must attempt at all events obeying them, tho' at the same time he acquaints me that Sir William Howe has sent him word that he has gone to Philadelphia, and indeed nothing Sir William says could give him reason to hope that any effort would be made in his favor."

The pitfalls of the split-strategy that should have been obvious to any half-awake mind ever since the communications of the previous March had finally dawned upon Germain by the end of

October; and by that time, of course, matters had gone awry beyond any possibility of recall and redemption.

Dogged Johnny Burgoyne, during that long pause at Fort Miller near Fort Edward on the upper Hudson, gathered to himself his cumbersome artillery train, drew some small reinforcements from Canada, and assembled supplies for a three-week campaign. While he was doing all this, his army was joined by a most unusual recruit. She was Frederika von Riedesel, the wife of Baron von Riedesel, the able commander of Burgoyne's German troops.

The baroness appeared upon the scene, riding in a *calèche* with her three small daughters, two maids, and a cook. She was a small, plump, pretty woman, with baby-blue eyes and Cupid's-bow lips. She was also determined and clever. Her bright eyes missed little, her keen mind understood what she saw, and she committed her observations to a diary that was to become invaluable for its account of conditions in the British camp.

Joining the army in the midst of a fierce campaign had been the Baroness von Riedesel's own decision. If camp followers could tag along, she could, too, she had informed her husband. "I told him I had sufficient health and pluck to undertake it, and that no matter what happened, he would never hear me murmur, but, on the contrary, I hoped to make myself useful to him on many occasions," she wrote.

She was not deceived by British rationalizations that Bennington had been a little affair that did not matter too much. She called it "this unfortunate event" that "paralyzed at once our operations." Nor was she at all taken in by the personality-boy side of Gentleman Johnny. Burgoyne had ordered his officers to divest themselves of all unnecessary equipment and travel light, an instruction that he blithely ignored himself. There were those thirty precious carts devoted to carrying luxuries necessary to let him live in the wilderness in the sportive fashion befitting an English gentleman on a country hunt.

The general had established himself in Duer's House at Fort Miller, and Baroness von Riedesel noted acidly: "It is very true that General Burgoyne likes to make himself easy and that he spent half his nights in singing and drinking and diverting himself with . . . his mistress . . . who was as fond of champagne as himself."

While Gentleman Johnny nerved himself for his final ordeal in such fashion, the fortunes of war were changing on the American side. George Washington had spent an apprehensive spring. He knew that Howe had an overwhelmingly powerful army of some 23,000 trained and disciplined troops, equipped with all the arms and supplies any general could want; and Washington simply could not imagine that Howe could be so stupid as not to recognize where the main chance lay and campaign up the Hudson.

When Washington learned on July 8 that Howe was embarking troops on British ships in New York Harbor, he fully expected that it was for a move up the Hudson to force a passage past American forts on the Hudson highlands. After the fall of Ticonderoga, Washington wrote that Howe's "designs . . . are most unquestionably against the Highlands." On July 24, when he learned that Howe had set sail the previous day with some 16,000 troops aboard 245 transports guarded by 16 warships, Washington was still convinced that this powerful expedition must be intended for the Hudson River campaign. It was true that he had been informed Howe had sailed not up the Hudson but out to sea past Sandy Hook; but Washington reasoned that this might be just a clever feint, designed to draw him out of position to the south. He was haunted by a nightmare vision that had Howe turning his fleet around and charging back up the Hudson. "Howe's in a manner abandoning General Burgoyne is so unaccountable a matter that till I am fully assured it is so, I cannot help casting my eyes continually behind me," Washington wrote.

Even though his own army was a pitiful, ragamuffin force compared to Howe's 16,000 veteran troops, Washington was so sensitive to the threat from the north that he stripped himself of some of his best fighters, men he could ill spare, in the hope of turning back Burgoyne. The most important of the contingents he sent north was the superb rifle corps led by Daniel Morgan. When Morgan reached the American camp near Saratoga, he had only 331 effectives, with 36 more on the sick list—a puny force in numbers, but a mighty one in effectiveness.

Morgan's men, drawn from the frontiers of Pennsylvania, Western Maryland, Virginia, and what is now West Virginia, were the deadliest fighters of their day. They were sharpshooters all; they were as expert in woodcraft as any Indian; and they carried the most fearsome weapon of their day—the long rifle.

It is a popular misconception to think of American forces in the Revolution as composed largely of riflemen. They were not. The standard weapon on both sides was the musket; and the musket was deadly only at close-up range, from 65 to 75 yards. It could fire a ball 125 yards, but at that range the shot was so spent it could only bruise, not kill.

The long rifle, on the other hand, could be fired with pin-point accuracy at ranges up to 300 yards, an astounding distance for those times. It was, however, uniquely the weapon of the frontier, used by scouts and Indian fighters recruited from the fringes of the seaboard settlements. Dr. Thacher, who later pictured so vividly the retreat from Ticonderoga, had been in Washington's camp at Cambridge, Massachusetts, when Morgan's riflemen first joined up in 1775, and he described in his journal the impression that they made:

"They are remarkably stout and hearty men, many of them exceeding six feet in height," he wrote. "They are dressed in white frocks or rifle shirts and round hats. These men are remarkable for the accuracy of their aim, striking a mark with great certainty at 200 yards distance. At a review, a company of them while on quick advance fired their bullets into objects seven inches in diameter, at a distance of 250 yards."

By the time Morgan and his riflemen reached the American camp, the high command had changed, and so had the fortunes of the campaign. The dillydallying Gates had arrived on August 19 and taken command from Schuyler. Never was a new commander more indebted to his predecessor, and never was one less grateful. The truly desperate situation that had existed after

the fall of Ticonderoga had been turned completely around by
the rout of St. Leger and Stark's stunning victory at Bennington,
both in large part attributable to Schuyler's foresight and willingness to risk his own army for the chance of crippling Burgoyne on the flanks. As Nathanael Greene, Washington's greatest general, wrote in reference to Gates: "This Gentleman is
a mere child of fortune. The Foundation of all Northern Suc-
cesses was laid long before his arrival there!"

But Gates, having schemed his way to command, could not
be generous; he could be only spiteful and petty. Perhaps he
could never forget his own lowly birth, the way advancement
to higher command in the British Army had been denied him
because he did not have noble connections and influence; undoubtedly, he equated aristocratic Philip Schuyler with that
high-born officer caste in the British Army that he hated. And
so he took a small man's petty revenge. He cut Schuyler dead;
and when he called a council of war, he summoned everybody,
even the commander of the Albany County militia—but not
Philip Schuyler.

Schuyler himself was naturally bitter. In a letter to Gouverneur
Morris, the New York patriot, he complained that "my crime
consists in not being a New England man in principle, and
unless they alter theirs I hope I never shall be. Gen. Gates is
their idol because he is at their direction." Morris, sympathizing,
wrote: "The new Commander-in-Chief . . . may, if he please,
neglect to ask or disdain to receive advice. But those who know
him well, I am sure, will be convinced that he needs it."

One of those who quickly became so convinced was Benedict
Arnold, returning in triumph from his relief of Fort Stanwix.
Arnold and Schuyler, though they had little in common in
their characters, had always worked well together; Arnold was
a Schuyler partisan—and the more he saw of Gates, the more
partisan he became. So were sown the seeds of a fierce feud
that was almost to tear the American camp apart, inspiring a
controversy that has lasted to the present day.

Though Gates must have known of the friendship between
Arnold and Schuyler, he treated Arnold far differently than

he had the deposed former commander of the Northern Department. There were reasons for this. Arnold, with his fighting image, was a hero to the New England troops, the very faction that was most favorable to Gates. The successful relief of Stanwix had added to Arnold's laurels; and when he returned to camp, he brought 1200 men with him. For the moment, at least, he was a man to be placated.

Recognizing this, Gates gave Arnold command of the left wing of his army—the wing that, as it turned out, was to do the bulk of the fighting. He strengthened Morgan's rifle corps by adding it to 250 sharpshooters of the elite light infantry force commanded by Major Henry Dearborn, like Morgan and Arnold, a veteran of the costly Canadian campaign and, like them, a doughty fighter. Morgan's and Dearborn's forces were to form the advance corps of the army under Arnold's over-all command. Into the Vermont hills on the far right flank, Gates sent Major General Lincoln in the vain hope that he could get stubborn John Stark to co-operate with the main army.

Having made these dispositions, Gates looked for a strong position from which to wage a defensive battle. On September 8 he marched his army north from its camp near the mouth of the Mohawk River and examined the ground around Stillwater. He could find no favorable, fortifiable position here; but three miles north he came upon exactly what he wanted. He found a steep and thickly wooded bluff known as Bemis Heights after a man who had a tavern on the river bank. Here, on September 12, Gates's highly talented young Polish engineer, Colonel Thaddeus Kosciusko, began to throw up a line of entrenchments.

The Bemis Heights position had much to recommend it; and, like Ticonderoga, it had one potentially fatal flaw. The heights were thickly wooded and rose steeply between 200 and 300 feet, crowding close upon a narrow strip of land along the Hudson's banks. Here ran the one good road to the south and Albany. Breastworks were thrown up across this road; and, above them, on the heights, fortifications were built on three sides of a square, with the rear left open. The right side of the square ran to the northeast, following the contour of the heights

as they paralleled the river. Then the line angled straight across
the front of the heights and bent backward on the left. Each
face of the line was about three quarters of a mile long. The
front section looked out upon a lower stretch of ground, cut by
two ravines through which flowed separate arms of Mill Creek.
To get at the Americans, it would seem, Burgoyne would have
to plunge down the river road and thrust his neck into that
narrow defile swept by American guns from the heights, or he
would have to launch a direct frontal attack across Mill Creek
to storm the American lines—a prospect that raised the specter
of another Bunker Hill.

There was, however, another option. Strong as the American
position was, it had a weakness. Close to the entrenchments on
the left rose a high wooded knoll overlooking the American
position. Like Mount Defiance at Fort Ticonderoga, it had
been left unprotected; and if the British could seize it by a wide
flanking march through the dense and entangling woods, they
might place some of Burgoyne's precious artillery there and
sweep the American position at relatively little cost to themselves. It remained to be seen what Burgoyne would do.

Gentleman Johnny was faced with a number of hard choices.
On August 28, when a band of Mohawk Indians had straggled
in from Oswego, he had learned of St. Leger's defeat. He was
now utterly on his own. He had a last chance to retreat before
it was too late. But Gentleman Johnny would not give up. He
was possessed by the notion that he must drive forever forward.
The question then was: What route should he take?

He was on the east bank of the Hudson; Gates, on the west.
Albany was also on the west. The eastern road along the river
lay wide open; Burgoyne could take it without opposition. But
if he did, he would have to cross the Hudson eventually further
down, where the river would be wider and deeper and more
difficult to cross. Almost certainly, too, if he followed this
course, he would find the Americans in new positions, waiting
to oppose him. It seemed better to cross the river at once.

Burgoyne built a bridge of boats across the Hudson and
ordered his army forward. Baroness von Riedesel recorded:

"We cherished the sweet hope of a sure victory, and of coming into the 'promised land'; and when we passed the Hudson River, and General Burgoyne said, 'The English never lose ground,' our spirits were greatly exhilarated."

The British marched onward in colorful pageantry, like an army on parade. The advance, led by Simon Fraser, swept past Burgoyne on September 13, colors whipping in the breeze, bands playing, the troops stepping out like soldiers eager to meet the enemy. The Germans followed them across the river the following day. Then Burgoyne destroyed the bridge of boats behind him, severing his last link with his supply base in Canada.

He had taken the big gamble. He had crossed his Rubicon. There could be no turning back.

CHAPTER ELEVEN

The First Battle of Freeman's Farm

Burgoyne fumbled blindly forward. He knew the American forces were entrenched somewhere ahead of him, but he did not know exactly where they were or in what strength. This lack of information stemmed from the fact that he had lost almost all of his Indian contingent that had been the forward eyes and ears of his army.

Smarting from the Jane McCrea atrocity and the manner in which Gates had seized upon it to blacken his reputation, Burgoyne had tried to curb his free-roving Indian allies. This had made them unhappy. Furthermore, Bennington had convinced them that this campaign was going to be no lark; it might well be a disaster. Sizing up the situation in a council of war, they decided that it was high time to go home while they still had the chance; and so they decamped with all their scalps and booty, only some 80 out of the original 500 remaining with Burgoyne. Even those who remained had little stomach for the far-ranging scouting duties that would bring them into conflict with Morgan's dreaded, ever-active riflemen.

With his Indians useless, with his view of the landscape cut off by the towering woods through which he pressed, Burgoyne led some 6000 rank and file southward along the river road and over rough inland trails. The Americans had broken down the bridges over creeks that threaded through the area, and these had to be replaced as the army crawled along. On the morning of September 16, borne faintly on southerly breezes, the British heard the eerie sounds of morning drums beating in the unseen American camp. Realizing he must be getting close to the enemy, Burgoyne probed ahead with some 2000 men while the rest of his army labored on the bridges so necessary if he were to bring up the thirty-five cannon and six mortars he still hauled with him. Burgoyne's scouting expedition failed to find the Americans; and on September 17 his army moved slowly up to the heights of land north of the American position. There Burgoyne established his headquarters on the farm of a man named Swords.

The American army under Gates, some 7000 strong at this point, was lying behind its fortified line on Bemis Heights just four miles ahead, but Burgoyne still did not know just where they were or how close. That he was almost upon the rebels, however, he could no longer doubt. A party of soldiers, accompanied by some women camp followers, straggled off beyond his lines to dig some potatoes in a nearby field. They were surprised by an American patrol which opened fire upon them. The Americans killed and wounded fourteen and took some prisoners. This relatively trifling loss enraged Burgoyne, who issued a harsh order to put a stop to such foraging. He wrote:

"The Lieut. Genl. will no longer bear to lose Men, for the pitiful consideration of Potatoes, or Forage. The Life of the Soldier is the property of the King, and since neither friendly Admonitions, repeated Injunctions, nor Corporal punishments have effect, after what has happened, the Army is now to be informed, and it is not doubted the Commanding Officers will do it solemnly, that the first Soldier caught beyond the Advanced Centinels of the Army, will be instantly Hanged."

If Burgoyne was having his troubles, so were the Americans. Gates had dispatched Major General Lincoln to bring John Stark and his victorious Bennington militia to the main camp to bolster the American forces for the great battle now impending. But the Cantankerous Man proved as cantankerous as ever.

Stark had little love for Lincoln, who had denounced him to Congress for his "insubordination" for refusing to follow orders before the Battle of Bennington. Stark also felt that Lincoln's report on that battle had done insufficient justice to himself and his men. As a consequence, he was just as bitter as ever, if not more so, and he kept advancing all kinds of excuses for not obeying Gates's orders. His men had the "meazels," he said; he was ill himself; he had only 800 men under him anyway—and what good could they do? Finally, on the morning of September 18, he did march into Gates's camp, but this was a gesture more contemptuous than obedient. The enlistments of his men all expired on that very day; and, according to James Wilkinson, they "neither unpacked the baggage which they carried on their backs, nor laid down to repose." They simply informed Gates's officers that their time was up, stayed until nightfall—and then marched out of camp again. They were still close enough to hear the roar of guns when the first great battle erupted the following day; but, again according to Wilkinson, "not a man returned."

While Stark and his men were thus marching off in the wrong direction, Burgoyne decided to make his first test of the American lines. On the morning of September 19—a bright and sunny day with the leaves of the trees already brilliant with their first fall colors—the British moved forward in three widely separated columns. Burgoyne's maneuver was a complicated one and ran the risk that the divided wings of his army might be mauled one by one.

Baron von Riedesel and General Phillips, with some of the artillery, were to advance down the river road. They had some 1100 rank and file and comprised the left wing. Burgoyne himself, with a force of similar size, advanced over rough wagon tracks in the center. Off to the right, separated from both the other wings, Simon Fraser with some 2000 men headed the main thrust. Burgoyne's plan called for Fraser to make a wide sweep around a deep ravine until he had circled the American left under Arnold. This was the most exposed flank of the American position; and if it could be rolled up, the Americans might be forced back into the river.

The British dispositions were no secret to the Americans. Some of Morgan's sharp-eyed riflemen, perched in high treetops, watched the unfolding British advance as the sun shone down on vivid red uniforms and winked on the bright steel of bayonets. Their reports to American headquarters—"a small hovel not ten feet square" well in the rear of the center of the American line—touched off the first furious argument between Arnold and Gates.

Never were two men more unalike; never were two men better fashioned by nature to hate each other—cautious "Granny" Gates and impetuous, fire-eating Benedict Arnold. Gates had determined to sit and wait behind his fortified lines on Bemis Heights. Time, he argued correctly, was on his side. Burgoyne's provisions were limited; if he lost men in an assault on the American lines, he could not replace them. On the other hand, Gates expected more and more militia to flock to his colors—as, indeed, they did—and it simply made no sense, as he saw it, to risk throwing his raw troops against trained and experienced British and German regulars in the open field.

Arnold argued, on the contrary, that it was not an open field. It was heavily wooded country, ideal for the kind of sharpshooting, guerrilla tactics at which the Americans were so adept. "We ought to march out and attack them," Arnold cried. Gates must have shuddered at the thought. But Arnold would not be silenced. To wait to be attacked, he thought, might be suicidal. The British had that train of heavy artillery; if they were allowed to approach unopposed and bring their cannon into play, they might shell the Americans out of their line or batter them so they could be routed in a follow-up attack. If this happened, it could be utter disaster; there was no other defense line to fall back on. On the other hand, if the Americans were repulsed in the woods, they would still have their entrenchments; nothing vital would have been lost.

Neither Gates nor Arnold seems to have given any consideration, despite the lesson of Ticonderoga, to the menace of that unfortified hill looming so close above the American left. Though both generals seem to have been equally blind to what should have been an obvious danger, this feature of the battlefield seems, looking back, to give more validity to Arnold's strategy than to that of Gates. Had Fraser been allowed to sweep around to the left unopposed, had the British been given the opportunity to place batteries on that hill, the result might well have been different.

As it turned out, Arnold did not win his argument with Gates, but neither did he wholly lose it. A compromise was reached under which a reluctant Gates agreed to let Daniel Morgan and his riflemen see what could be accomplished by ambushing the British in the entangling woods. Morgan, who had heartily supported Arnold's arguments, rushed off to prepare for the battle.

Here was one of the most colorful figures on the battlefield of Saratoga. Big, strapping Dan Morgan, like so many of the riflemen he led, had been a hell-raiser much of his life. Born in New Jersey around 1735, he had quarreled with his father at seventeen and had left home and gone off to the western Virginia frontier. An habitual brawler, he was in his element among tough, brawling men.

He had been a teamster attached to the ill-fated expedition of the British General James Braddock, who had attempted to drive the French from the area around what is now Pittsburgh at the outset of the French and Indian War. Morgan and his fellow wagoners exasperated British officers by their colossal drinking, their never-ending brawls and their incessant affairs with Indian women. Once, when an officer reprimanded him for such combined misconduct, the fiery young Morgan, no respecter of rank, knocked the officer down. The result was a drumhead court-martial that, it is said, sentenced Morgan to the usually lethal penalty of 500 lashes on his bare back. Only a granite of a man could have survived that punishment, but Morgan did. He even quipped that the wielder of the lash had miscounted; he had laid on only 499 strokes instead of 500.

This brutal experience scarred Morgan's back for life and left him with a deep, abiding hatred of such punishments and of the British officer caste that countenanced them. He learned other lessons and learned them well. Like George Washington, he survived the French and Indian ambush that cut Braddock's force to ribbons, and he was impressed with the idiocy of the British system that kept soldiers standing in ordered ranks, firing by volleys, completely exposed to enemies picking them off at will from the shelter of surrounding trees—a method Morgan himself was to apply so well on this opening day of battle.

Following Braddock's defeat, Morgan had served with the Virginia Rangers and had again been almost killed. Indians ambushed him and two of his companions. The other two fell dead at the first fire, and Morgan himself was terribly wounded. A ball struck him in the back of the neck and tore completely through, shattering his left cheek and jaw. Almost unconscious, he fell forward on his horse; and, clutching his horse's mane, more dead than alive, he managed to outdistance his Indian pursuers.

Even such experiences had not taken the roisterer out of Morgan. He brawled in taverns and was constantly hounded for not paying his liquor bills and his card debts. But eventually he had settled down. He formed a common-law alliance with sixteen-year-old Abigail Curry, acquired a farm, and purchased a few slaves. The roisterer began to become a solid citizen, and by 1771 he had been made a captain of militia. By the time he led his riflemen to join Washington at Cambridge, he was an experienced handler of men, and he had perfected a novel system of summoning and directing his riflemen on the battle-field. He had a small instrument that woodsmen used to imitate a turkey's call, a frontier method of decoying wild turkeys into rifle range, and it was this turkey-gobbler call that was now to haunt the British in what was to become known as the First Battle of Freeman's Farm.

It was about one o'clock in the afternoon before the British were ready to strike. Fraser, with the strongest force, was well along on his wide sweep in the hope of circling the American left. Burgoyne himself, leading the center, pressed over a bridge across what was to become known as "the great ravine" and marched up a slope to a jutting knob of land, crowned by a cleared fifteen-acre patch of farmland, surrounded by dense woods, that had belonged to a farmer named Freeman. A forward patrol of Burgoyne's advancing center came out of the woods and deployed in the open about Freeman's abandoned log cabin—and, suddenly, the forest walls burst into a flame of rifle fire. Dan Morgan's terrible "shirtmen" were on target; every British officer except one, and many of the men in the clearing, fell dead or wounded. With a whoop, the headstrong riflemen left the cover of the woods and charged after them—and so ran headlong into the bulk of Burgoyne's advancing center corps.

The disorganized riflemen were in turn thrown back; and for a moment it seemed disaster threatened. Morgan, beside himself with anger and vexation, stood behind the center of his line, just two aides beside him. And now, above the crackle of scattered musketry and rifle fire, there sounded for the first time, loud and clear, the call of the turkey gobbler. It was as effective as any signal beaten out on a drum. Morgan's riflemen heard and heeded, fell back to join him and regroup. Dearborn's light infantry came to their aid, and Arnold, the spirit of the battlefield, threw in regiment after regiment from his left-wing command post.

A dispute has raged ever since about Arnold's precise role on this day. Was he actually, personally, involved in the battle— or wasn't he? The unscrupulous James Wilkinson (later, as an American general, he was to become known as one of the great rogues of history, his itching fingers unable to resist the bribe of Spanish gold) insisted in his account of the battle that Arnold was never personally on the field. Gates and his coterie all took up the chorus, and many historians have followed their lead. But such experts in American history as Henry Steele Commager and Richard B. Morris have concluded that "the overwhelming evidence is the other way."

One of the most vivid pieces of that evidence is contained in

the recollections of Captain E. Wakefield of Dearborn's light
infantry, who was on the field throughout the battle. Wakefield
later wrote:

"I shall never forget the opening scene of the first day's conflict. The riflemen and light infantry were ordered to clear the
woods of the Indians. Arnold rode up, and with his sword
pointing to the enemy emerging from the timber, addressing
Morgan, he said, 'Colonel Morgan, you and I have seen too
many redskins to be deceived by that garb of paint and feathers;
they are asses in lions' skins, Canadians and Tories; let your
riflemen cure them of their borrowed plumes.'

"And so they did; for in less than fifteen minutes the 'Wagon
Boy,' with his Virginia riflemen, sent the painted devils with
a howl back to the British lines. Morgan was in his glory,
catching the inspiration of Arnold, as he thrilled his men;
when he hurled them against the enemy, he astonished the
English and Germans with the deadly fire of his rifles.

"Nothing could exceed the bravery of Arnold on this day; he
seemed the very genius of war. Infuriated by the conflict and
maddened by Gates' refusal to send reinforcements, which he
repeatedly called for, and knowing he was meeting the brunt of
the battle, he seemed inspired with the fury of a demon."

Wakefield's account matches everything that is known of
Arnold; it is almost impossible to imagine him waiting in a
command post behind the lines, as Gates did, when there was
a battle to be fought. And never was battle waged more fero-
ciously in a confined space than the one that now raged back
and forth across the 350 yards of Freeman's clearing.

Arnold hurled two regiments of New Hampshire Continentals
into the fray, extending Morgan's line to the left. There, on high
ground shrouded in forest, Simon Fraser, unable to complete his
encircling march because of the premature outbreak of firing,
had taken up a defensive position. But there was a gap between
his wing of the army and Burgoyne's center. On the other flank,
on the British left down by the river, General Phillips heard
the roar of musketry and rifle fire and came dashing to Burgoyne's aid, dragging four fieldpieces with him. Around these,

the British formed a line, with three regiments facing the Americans.

There was a brief lull while these reinforcements on both sides were getting into position; but between two and three o'clock, according to Lieutenant William Digby of the Shropshire Regiment, the fighting was resumed in even more fierce and desperate fashion. "Such an explosion of fire I never had any idea of before," he wrote, "and the heavy artillery joining in concert like great peals of thunder, assisted by the echoes of the woods, almost deafened us with the noise."

It was a confused, milling battle; but the heart of it raged back and forth across the narrow clearing of Freeman's Farm. The Americans, on their left, collided with the forces of Fraser and contained them. Arnold, ever aggressive, probed for a soft spot and found it in that gap between the British right and center. He drove the New Hampshire Continentals deep into it, then "countermarched" his men to attack Burgoyne's forces in the clearing. This forced the British to extend and sweep back their lines, a maneuver that brought one of their regiments, the 62nd, under fire on both flanks.

All the time Morgan's riflemen were doing deadly execution. Some of them were perched high in the treetops, their rifle shirts almost indistinguishable among the autumn leaves, and from these vantage points they directed an unerring fire at the exposed British troops in the clearing. British officers and the gunners manning the artillery were their special targets. So deadly was the riflemen's fire that the artillerymen fell in dead and wounded heaps around their guns, and the guns themselves were silenced.

Time and again, the British were driven back across the clearing by the withering hail that swept their ranks. Then the Americans would charge, seize the guns, and try to turn them around on the British. But before they could fire, the British troops came charging back again with the bayonet, driving the Americans into the encircling woods. Six times such charges and countercharges swept across the clearing, and the piles of the dead and wounded mounted. "Senior officers who had witnessed the hardest fighting of the Seven Years' War declared they had never experienced so long and hot a fire," a British historian later wrote.

The 62nd Regiment, battered from two sides, was punished with special severity. Its ranks were decimated; it almost broke. When it tried one final bayonet charge, it lost twenty-five men as prisoners. Burgoyne's situation was getting desperate. His ammunition was running low; his ranks were being winnowed in appalling fashion. Arnold was convinced that only a little more force was needed to cave in the wavering British center and destroy Burgoyne's entire army. He whirled away, riding furiously to Gates's headquarters to plead for more troops to deliver the knockout blow.

Gates, cautious to the end, "deemed it prudent not to weaken" his lines. But finally he yielded enough to Arnold's pleadings to order Brigadier General Ebenezer Learned's brigade forward. By so doing, however, Gates robbed the action of any effect it might have had. All the evidence seems to indicate that the "old midwife" was horrified by Arnold's performance. Arnold had thrown in his whole command, and by so doing had committed the American forces to the kind of major engagement Gates wanted to shun. There was also in Gates's mind, by all accounts, a residue of distrust of Arnold's judgment stemming from what Gates considered his disregard of orders and his rash conduct at the Battle of Valcour Island the year before. In the circumstances, considering the personalities of the two men, it is little wonder that Gates was almost in a panic at the thought of what this madman might do next.

Such were the undercurrents that were working as Learned's brigade moved off. The commanders could see nothing of the battle from Gates's headquarters, so completely did the surrounding forest screen off the action; but just at this juncture, an aide came riding up to Gates to tell him the battle was still undecided, though it seemed to be going well. "My God, I will soon put an end to it," Arnold cried, putting spurs to his horse.

Gates ordered Wilkinson to stop him, giving Arnold positive orders to remain behind the American lines. Arnold, chafing, obeyed. And Learned's brigade, without him to direct them, blundered in the woods, lost their way, and clashed with Fraser's corps. They never did get where they were supposed to have gone—into that perilous gap in the British line where Arnold had intended to fling them.

On the British side, the commanders in the field were more decisive. Down by the river road, the able Baron von Riedesel, hearing the incessant roar of desperate battle, knew and made the right move. He ordered his German troops to leave their line of march and hurry to Burgoyne's assistance. He led them all and came charging on the field at the end of the day while the fight was "raging at its fiercest." He was barely in time. As he later wrote: "The three brave English regiments had been, by the steady fire of fresh relays of the enemy, thinned down to one-half and now formed a small band surrounded by heaps of dead and wounded."

Not waiting for his whole force to arrive, Riedesel called on two of his companies to charge at once. "With drums beating and his men shouting, 'Hurrah,'" a British soldier wrote, "he attacked the enemy on the double-quick." The Americans, caught off balance by this sudden and vigorous charge, fell back into the woods. Riedesel's Hesse-Hanau artillerymen dragged two six-pounders into position and fired a hail of grapeshot at their retreating foes, and Riedesel's own regiment, coming into action, followed this up with a heavy volley of musketry.

That was virtually the end of the battle. Riedesel had arrived in time to save the day. It was now dark; the Americans, unable to grasp the victory Arnold had sought, drew off and retreated to their fortifications on Bemis Heights a mile away. The British camped where they stood on the hard-fought field. Technically, since they held the ground, they might claim a victory, but it was a victory that had all but destroyed them.

The regiments in Burgoyne's center had been mauled almost beyond recognition. The embattled 62nd, which had gone into action 350 strong, came out of it with only 60 men and 5 officers. Though only about 1000 of Burgoyne's troops had been steadily engaged, his over-all losses were staggering—some 600 killed, wounded or captured. The Americans, on the other hand, had lost only 65 killed, 218 wounded, and 33 missing, and these losses could be more than offset by fresh militia forces that were arriving almost every day.

The shock to the British was profound. The battered troops spent a sleepless night, lying on their arms, their ears filled, as Lieutenant Digby wrote, with "the groans of our wounded and dying at a small distance." Lieutenant Anburey, writing several weeks later, reflected: "The courage and obstinacy with which the Americans fought were the astonishment of everyone, and we now became fully convinced that they are not the contemptible enemy we had hitherto imagined them . . ."

On the American side there was both exultation and frustration. There was exultation over a battle that had damaged Burgoyne almost beyond hope of recovery; frustration, because the great opportunity for a complete and smashing victory had been missed. Major Dearborn reflected the first feeling when he wrote: "I trust that we have now convinced the British butchers that the 'cowardly' Yankees can, and where there is a call for it, will fight."

Yet many felt, like Arnold, that the American army had failed to seize the victory that had been within its grasp. Christopher Ward, one of the best military historians of the Revolution, was to write much later: "The incapacity of Gates as commander of a fighting force was convincingly demonstrated that day." Had it not been for Arnold and Morgan, Gates would have huddled in his lines, and Fraser would have been left unhindered to make his engulfing sweep against the vulnerable American left. And throughout the battle Gates had kept the vast bulk of his army, more than 4000 troops, sitting on their hands behind their entrenchments. When Riedesel had rushed off to save Burgoyne, he had left the British artillery train and all of the army's provisions on the river road, with only a thin screen of troops to protect them; but the American right wing, which could have swarmed over the lot by a determined thrust, had been kept under such a tight leash by Gates that it had sat and watched and fired not a single shot.

Arnold was convinced—and rightly—that he and Morgan and the regiments of his left wing, alone and unaided, had battled the British Army to a standstill. And when Gates, petty as ever, failed to mention either Arnold or Morgan in his report of the battle, leaving the impression that he alone deserved the credit, there erupted in the American camp a new controversy, fueled by emotions as fierce and passionate as any that had animated the soldiers in this First Battle of Freeman's Farm.

CHAPTER TWELVE

Gates and Arnold

THE GUNS had hardly fallen silent after the furious battle of September 19 when there erupted in the American camp the first of those incredible and angry scenes that were to set Gates and Arnold at each other's throats. The protagonist in this opening act was Colonel Richard Varick, an aide on Gates's staff but a partisan of the deposed Philip Schuyler. Varick's sympathies at the time are clear from a note he wrote to Schuyler three days later. In this, he said: "This I am certain of, that Arnold has all the credit for the action of the 19th, for he was ordering out troops to it, while the other [Gates] was in Dr. Pott's tent backbiting his neighbors."

The "backbiting" apparently continued at Gates's dining table on the evening of the battle. Gates apparently made some slurring reference to Arnold. We do not know what it was, for Varick wrote only that he took offense at "words that dropped from Gates." This was putting it mildly. Varick took such offense, indeed, that he jumped to his feet, screamed to his commander in chief that he was resigning as muster master of the army, and added furiously, unpardonably, that he would rather see Gates "drawn and quartered" than serve under him a minute longer.

In any well-ordered army, an officer who offered such insult

to his commander would find himself under instant arrest and
facing a court-martial; but the Continental Army was gov-
erned by no such military protocol. It was a loose collection
of volunteer soldiers, and discipline, what there was of it,
depended more upon the soldiers' willingness to give their allegiance to a commander they trusted than it did upon the
privileges of rank. And so Varick, having flung his insult,
stalked out of Gates's tent; and Gates let him go. But the
initial damage had been done.

Worse quickly followed. Varick rushed directly from Gates to
Arnold. He found Arnold brooding darkly in his quarters about
the frustrations of the day of battle. The repeated arguments
with Gates, his inability to get Gates to *fight,* the way Gates
had confined him to camp as Learned's men blundered off, the
failure to seize a victory that had been there for the taking—all
of this rankled the fierce, tempestuous, supersensitive soul of
Benedict Arnold. He was as primed for an explosion as a
powder keg with a slow fuse burning; and at this moment
Varick burst in upon him to supply the only needed spark.
Varick told Arnold what had just taken place at Gates's table,
and Arnold responded by appointing the young colonel who
had just insulted the commander in chief to his own personal
staff. Thus was insult piled upon insult. And Gates was just the
man to take any petty revenge he could.

In his report of the battle, he at least evened the score. He
attributed the victory to a nameless "detachment" of his army.
This was carrying pettiness to an extreme. It is standard operat-
ing procedure for a commander in chief to recognize the services
of men who have fought valiantly. In a battle like that which
had just concluded, the commander bathes in the reflected glory
in any event, and the least he can do for the morale of his
own men is to commend those who have behaved bravely and
well. But Gates, in his spitefulness, could not do the decent, the
common-sense thing—and Arnold was beside himself with rage.

He felt that Gates had deliberately cheated him of the glory
that should have been his, and any man who cheated Arnold
of his cherished glory reaped a human tempest. In a fury,

Arnold charged into headquarters on the night of September 22. There he and Gates engaged in a word brawl, almost loud enough for Burgoyne's outposts to hear. Colonel Henry Brockholst Livingston, another ardent Schuyler fan, witnessed the encounter and later wrote to Schuyler: "Matters were altercated in a very high strain. Both were warm, the latter [Gates] rather passionate and very assuming. Towards the end of the debate Mr. Gates told Arnold, 'He did not know of his being a Major General. He had sent his resignation to Congress. [This referred to Arnold's earlier action when he had protested other officers' being jumped over his head, a deed he had reconsidered.] He [Gates] had never given him [Arnold] command of any division of the army. Genl. Lincoln would be here in a day or two, that then he should have no occasion for him, and would give him a pass to go to Philadelphia, whenever he choose it.'"

This was contempt, utter and complete. Arnold, the firebrand, shouted he would not "brook such usage" and stormed out, slamming the headquarters' door in Gates's face. He was charging away, a human thundercloud, when whom should he see, riding into camp on an old nag that could hardly bear his weight but the corpulent General Lincoln himself. The general with whom Gates had threatened to replace him was on the scene ahead of time and available for the post.

Arnold returned to his own quarters where, it appears, he reviewed what had happened with Varick and Livingston. Both were such ardent and prejudiced Schuyler men that they seem to have rejoiced at the vendetta between the two top generals in the American camp; and it may be, as many have speculated, that they egged Arnold on. Given Arnold's own fiery nature, however, it seems unlikely that he needed much urging. He sat down immediately and penned a long letter to Gates. It was not a respectful letter, but for Arnold, in the rage that possessed him, it was comparatively mild.

Arnold began by refuting Gates's wholly ridiculous statement that he had not been in command of a division. He cited the troops that had been placed under him, including those of

Morgan and Dearborn, in the division that had indeed formed the left wing of the army. He recited the events of the battle of the nineteenth, the manner in which he had found it necessary "to send out the whole of my division," the fact that no other troops had done anything of consequence. Then he came to the heart of his grievance:

"I have been informed that in the returns transmitted to Congress of the killed and wounded in the action the troops were mentioned as a detachment of the army, and in orders of this day [September 22] I observe it is mentioned that Colonel Morgan's corps not being in any brigade or division of this army are to make returns and reports only to head quarters, from whence they are alone to receive orders, altho it is notorious to the whole army that they have been in and done duty with my division for some time past."

Arnold concluded that, as Gates "thought me of so little consequence to this army," he had decided to join General Washington, with whom he might "possibly have it in my power to serve my country, tho I am thought of no consequence in this Department." He asked for a pass for himself; his two aides, Livingston and Varick; and three servants.

Gates replied, again with cold contempt, on September 23. "You wrote me nothing last Night but what had been sufficiently altercated between us in the Evening," he told Arnold. Relations between the two had now deteriorated to the point that Arnold even bickered about the kind of a pass Gates sent—and so Gates sent him "a common pass" so that he could leave as soon as he chose.

Now that Arnold was free to go, however, he would not. He knew that the business with Burgoyne was yet to be settled. There would have to be another battle; this meant another chance for glory. And so, though he had been deprived of his command, though he had asked permission to leave and been granted it, he stayed on—and still insisted that he commanded the left wing of the army. When he came upon General Lincoln giving orders to his troops, he told Lincoln to get over to the right wing where he belonged. He still commanded the left,

Arnold said, and he instructed Lincoln to tell Gates he had said so. Lincoln departed. Gates did nothing. He simply ignored Arnold.

Word of the feud and Arnold's threat to leave spread through the army and "has caused great uneasiness among the soldiery," Livingston informed Schuyler in one letter. In another, he wrote that Arnold "enjoys the confidence and affection of officers and soldiers. They would, to a man, follow him to conquest or death. His absence will dishearten them to such a degree as to render them of but little service." And so an effort now began to persuade Arnold to stay.

Livingston informed Schuyler that "General [Enoch] Poor proposed an Address from the general officers and colonels in his division, returning him [Arnold] thanks for his past service and particularly for his conduct during the late action and requesting his stay. The Address was framed, and consented to by Poor's officers. Those of Gen. Learned refused. They acquiesced in the propriety of the measure, but were afraid of giving umbrage to General Gates."

Receiving these communiqués, Schuyler became greatly disturbed. He was not delighted, as Livingston and Varick seemed to be, but filled with concern for the larger issue—what might happen if, as he wrote, the army were left entirely in Gates's hands by the departure of Arnold, whom he called "that gallant officer." The implied rebuke to Schuyler's overenthusiastic young friends was clear. A bit crestfallen, they went to work and drafted a far milder "address," one that did not even mention Arnold's role in the action of the nineteenth, but simply implored him to stay for the good of the army. This was signed by all the general officers except Lincoln and Gates.

While the American high command was thus embroiled, Burgoyne missed his golden chance for victory. The troops in Arnold's command, who had borne the whole action of the nineteenth, were exhausted and short of powder and musket balls. In the whole American army, there were less than forty rounds of ammunition per man, not nearly enough for a prolonged engagement. So critical was the shortage that back in

Albany Philip Schuyler went around collecting lead from window frames and sending it to Bemis Heights to be melted down into gun pellets. Burgoyne's army, on the other hand, was plentifully supplied at this point. Sixty rounds of ammunition per man were issued to the troops on the morning of September 20, and plans were made to renew the assault.

Burgoyne sent his sick, his wounded, and the women and children back to his base camp by the river. There they were to be guarded while the rest of his army, some 5000 men, was concentrated in one driving column whose purpose would be to complete the sweep around the American left that Fraser had started the previous day. This was still the danger spot, the critical weakness in the American position; and even Wilkinson later admitted that it was "highly probable" a determined thrust at this time "would have gained a decisive victory."

The Americans expected that the battle would be renewed momentarily, and they awaited it with considerable dread. There is some evidence that Gates was more prepared for retreat than for battle and victory. Sergeant Ephraim Squire of the Connecticut Line kept noting in his diary almost daily orders making the army ready to decamp. On September 20 he wrote: "Today ordered to strike our tents at 3 o'clock p.m. hourly expecting the enemy to force our lines." On September 21: "Sunday. Much expecting the enemy, struck tents ready to march." And as late as September 24: "Today ordered to strike our tents."

But Burgoyne, usually the most stubborn of men, wavered at the very moment when stubbornness might have been his one redeeming virtue. After making preparations to renew battle on the twentieth, he did not. His hospitals were full, and he apparently felt his magazines and supplies were inadequately guarded. He therefore postponed action for another day; and then on September 21, providentially for the Americans, he received a communication that changed everything.

A courier from Sir Henry Clinton in New York slipped through the American lines with a coded message. It was dated September 11 and read:

"You know my good will and are not ignorant of my poverty.

If you think 2000 men can assist you effectually, I will make a push at Montgomery [one of the American forts guarding the Hudson highlands] in about ten days. But ever jealous of my flanks if they make a move in force on either of them I must return to save this important post. I expect reinforcements every day. Let me know what you wish."

It was certainly not a bold letter nor did it promise much. Sir Henry Clinton, who had been left in New York with a sizable army at his command, was one of those worry-wort generals who always feared that some great disaster might happen to him if he dared greatly. Washington's weak Continental Army had been drawn to the south to battle Howe for Philadelphia, and there was hardly a company of militia left to "menace" New York. But Clinton kept looking fearfully over his shoulder, worrying lest Washington, by some unexplained magic, might suddenly materialize out of the skies to descend upon New York if Clinton dared venture in force up the Hudson. What he offered Burgoyne, then, was little more than a demonstration against the American forts on the lower river; but Burgoyne, by a miscalculation it is difficult to understand, snatched at this timorous offer as if it represented genuine rescue from the south.

Ever since the shock of Bennington and the defeat of St. Leger, Burgoyne had been grasping at a frail straw; he had been looking for a miracle—the sudden emergence of the British Army in New York for a drive up the Hudson to Albany. Clearly, Clinton was not proposing such a full-scale effort, and Burgoyne understood that he was not for he replied to Clinton: "An attack, or the menace of an attack, upon Montgomery, must be of great use, as it will draw away part of this force, and I will follow them close. Do it my dear friend directly."

Then Burgoyne sat down to wait, the worst thing he could possibly have done. His belief that even "the menace of an attack" would help him was sheer delusion. Time, that long line of communication with Canada now virtually abandoned, approaching winter—everything was against him. Without a major attack up the Hudson, something that Clinton certainly did not promise, Burgoyne was strictly on his own; and if he had any chance to avoid complete disaster, he had to strike in full force and quickly. This Burgoyne did not do.

Gates, whatever his faults, sized up the strategic situation much more astutely. He knew that time was his greatest ally. While Burgoyne began to build three strong redoubts to fortify his line running from the river across Freeman's Farm and on to a small height of land to the north, Gates sat behind his fortified lines of Bemis Heights and waited for time to work its miracle. Day by day, it did. Day by day, more farmers left their fields and, toting their own guns, joined Gates's ranks, swelling his army by October 7 to a force of some 11,000 men, more than double the number that Burgoyne had.

The fatal pause, the wasting delay, had robbed Burgoyne of any chance he might have had, and the noose began to tighten now about his isolated army.

CHAPTER THIRTEEN

The Riflemen

GENTLEMAN JOHNNY BURGOYNE now learned about frontier fighting the hard way. While he fortified his camp and waited, the Americans buzzed close around him, swarming like the insects in the forest. Morgan's riflemen and the band of Oneida Indians who had joined Gates gave him no peace. The British troops dared not venture beyond their fortified lines; sometimes they were not even safe within them. Day and night, rifle bullets spattered the British camp, picking off any sentry who exposed himself.

Lieutenant Anburey described the situation in his journal. He wrote that "not a night passes but there is firing and continual attacks upon the advanced pickets especially those of the Germans." The soldiers learned to eat and sleep though the gunfire was "very near them," but the officers "rest in their clothes, and the field officers are up frequently in the night."

One of the American patrols infiltrated the British lines and got 500 yards behind British headquarters. There they surprised a group of soldiers digging potatoes and carried them off as prisoners "in the very faces of their comrades."

Dan Morgan's riflemen were in their element, flitting like ghosts through the dense surrounding forests, penning up

Burgoyne's badgered army, constantly sniping, giving the British no peace. Among this tough resourceful breed, one man began to stand out above all others as the supreme wilderness scout, the greatest of Indian fighters. He was Timothy Murphy, and he was to become a living legend. Before the war was over, he was as famous in the Mohawk and Schoharie valleys of Upper New York State as Daniel Boone was in Kentucky.

Murphy had been born of Irish parents in the wild region of New Jersey's northern Sussex County, then virtually a part of the frontier. He was relatively short, estimates placing his height at between five feet six and five feet nine; but he was solidly built, had great muscular strength, and was noted for his endurance and fleetness of foot. His naturally dark complexion had been tanned by constant exposure until he was as bronzed as any Indian. His hair was black, and he had piercing dark eyes in a square-set, determined face.

All of Morgan's riflemen were remarkable sharpshooters, but legend has it that Timothy Murphy was the deadliest of them all. Modesty was never one of Tim's virtues, and in later life he became positively insulted when anyone suggested he might ever have missed a shot. Whatever the truth of this, two things are beyond question: Timothy Murphy was an exceptional marksman, and he carried the most unusual weapon of his day—a double-barreled long rifle.

It is not quite clear how this novel weapon came to be created. Apparently Tim had it made especially for himself by James Golcher, of Easton, Pennsylvania, one of the best-known gunsmiths of his day. There had been double-barreled rifles before Tim Murphy came along—some of them are still preserved in museums—but these had been cumbersome, awkward, curiosity pieces; Tim's double-barreled long rifle was entirely different. It was light enough to be carried on long treks over wilderness trails, and many an Indian who leaped at Tim after he had fired one barrel, believing him defenseless, discovered in the few seconds left him on earth that the second barrel was as deadly as the first.

Tim Murphy had been in the thick of the First Battle of

Freeman's Farm, and in the lull afterward he and his insepara-
ble companion, David Elerson, teamed up in a series of light-
ning forays that made them the talk of Morgan's camp. Twice
they cut off British foraging parties, shooting or driving off their
guards and bringing the supplies the foragers had gathered into
the American camp. On another occasion, they stole up at night
so close to the British lines that they surprised and captured a
sentinel. From him they learned the British password, and it
seemed to Tim a pity not to use it.

Telling Elerson to take the captured sentinel in, Tim walked
boldly into the British camp. When pickets challenged him, he
gave the proper countersign. He was apparently mistaken in
the dark for a Tory follower. Undeterred and unchecked, he
roamed the camp until he spotted a lighted tent, with the
silhouette of a British officer cast against the canvas. The officer
was seated at a camp desk, writing a letter. Circling to the rear
of the tent, Tim wriggled inside under the canvas, as noiseless
as a snake. The British officer had no idea he was no longer
alone until he felt the prick of a knife at the back of his neck
and a menacing voice said in his ear: "Don't make a sound or
I'll butcher you."

Tim prodded the helpless British officer to his feet and suggested they take a stroll in the nice night air. Together, with
the constant prick of Tim's knife serving as a reminder to the
officer to behave, they walked out of the camp. When pickets
challenged, Tim gave the proper password, and he and his
officer "friend" strolled beyond the lines, down the dip of
ground, across the ravine, and up the opposite slope to the
American entrenchments on Bemis Heights. There Tim turned
the Briton over to his superior officers, and Morgan himself
came to interrogate the prisoner.

Deeds like these made Tim Murphy's a name that was on
every tongue—and his most important single feat was yet to be
performed.

Even as Tim Murphy and the rest of Morgan's riflemen were
driving Burgoyne to distraction with their constant sniping,
disaster was striking his rear—that long, broken line of com-

munication that ran back up the lakes through Fort Ticonderoga to Canada, the only possible source of aid or route of retreat.

General Lincoln, who had been given supervision over the right flank across the river, had gathered a considerable force of militia in the Vermont hills. Learning that Burgoyne had only a small garrison at Ticonderoga, Lincoln dispatched three raiding parties of 500 men each to play hob with the British supply lines. One force occupied Skenesborough, which had been abandoned by the British. Another demonstrated against Mount Independence, and a third, led by Colonel John Brown, made a surprise attack on Ticonderoga itself.

Brown, in his sweep up the lakes, first mopped up a small British garrison that had been left at Fort George. Then he pressed on north and circled cautiously about Ticonderoga. His men lay hidden in the woods for two days, watching the fort and perfecting their plans. They went undiscovered, and on September 18 Brown stunned the British garrison of about 900 men by a sudden sortie. He stormed the old French lines, captured the blockhouse guarding the sawmills, and overwhelmed the British outpost on Mount Defiance.

He had no cannon with which to bombard the fort from Defiance, and his force was too small to penetrate the main defenses. But he succeeded, by his sudden dash, in freeing 100 American prisoners and capturing 315 British troops. Bluffing magnificently, he called upon the commander of the fort to surrender, but this demand was rejected. Still Brown did not hurry away. He lurked about Ticonderoga for four more days, destroying 200 bateaux, seventeen armed sloops, and a large quantity of stores. Then, on September 22, having accomplished all that he could, he marched off with his long file of prisoners.

Word of Brown's feat reached the American camp on Bemis Heights on September 21 and touched off an outburst of rejoicing that had the British puzzled. Burgoyne's troops could hear the lusty cheering of the Americans and the thirteen guns that were fired in salute of some momentous victory. But it was a week before they learned the cause. And even then they got the

news only because Gates released a prisoner, Cornet Graef of
the German dragoons, who let Burgoyne in on the secret.

Everything was now going wrong for Gentleman Johnny.
Brown's raid on his communications showed that he was
virtually cut off from Canada, and the news from the south was
even worse.

Sir Henry Clinton, who had been left to hold New York with
some 7000 troops, about 3000 of them Tories, had received
heavy reinforcements from England on September 24. These
brought his command up to some 10,000 men, nearly 7000 of
them regulars—2700 British troops and 4200 German mer-
cenaries.

It would seem that a daring commander might have used this
strong army to co-operate with Burgoyne, putting pressure on
Gates from both front and rear; but Clinton was not a daring
commander. He even called himself "a shy bitch." And so,
timorous as ever, he organized an expedition of some 4000
men, including some Tories, to make a half-hearted stab up
the Hudson at the American forts guarding the highlands about
forty miles north of New York. Fort Clinton stood on the
northeast shoulder of Bear Mountain on the west side of the
river; and, across a ravine, half a mile distant, stood Fort
Montgomery. The two forts commanded the twisting river channel, here only half a mile wide.

Clinton's thrust met with such swift and complete success that
one can only wonder what a more determined commander might
have achieved. Having lured the Americans out of position by a
feint toward the east side of the Hudson, Clinton landed his
troops at Stony Point, and in one day's fighting seized both
American forts. Fort Constitution on the east side of the river,
slightly higher up, was abandoned without a fight; a boom that
had been thrown across the river was broken; and a small flotilla
of American ships that had sheltered behind it were burned to
prevent their falling into British hands. As Clinton wrote
Burgoyne in the heady moment of victory, there was "nothing
between us now but Gates."

Even this "nothing" was too much for the timid Sir Henry

Clinton. He had never contemplated making so daring a move as an all-out drive toward Albany; the most he had envisioned, as he had written Burgoyne earlier, was a diversion against the American forts on the Hudson highlands. He had now completed that diversion with unexpected ease and great success, and, as far as he was concerned, this marked the whole of his contribution. Also, just at this time, he received an order from Howe, who had taken Philadelphia, calling for reinforcements, and this order gave Clinton the only excuse he needed to abandon the whole Hudson River campaign.

During the drive up the Hudson, Clinton had learned of Burgoyne's increasingly desperate situation. Two messengers had reached him after slipping through the American lines. They bore a short note from Burgoyne in response to Clinton's letter of September 11—a joyous note urging Clinton to hurry and fall upon the Americans' rear—and they gave Clinton verbal descriptions of the plight of Burgoyne's weakened army. Still, Clinton felt that he had done all he could; and in a letter to Burgoyne dated October 6—a message that was never delivered because the courier carrying it was captured and executed— Clinton told Burgoyne that he could not presume to give him orders as to the best course for him to follow. And he added, on an injured note, that "he thinks it impossible General Burgoyne could really suppose Sir Henry Clinton had any idea of penetrating to Albany with the small force he mentioned to him in his letter of the 11th of September."

Clinton's move up the Hudson had been in any event too little and too late; and before the end of the month, shortly after the final disaster had overtaken Burgoyne, the British forces melted away down river to New York.

Burgoyne, hearing nothing from Clinton, realized that his army was almost entrapped. His rear was being raided; from the south, where he had hoped for rescue, there was only ominous silence. He had to make a crucial decision. The sensible thing, as some of his officers thought, would have been to try to fight his way back to Fort Ticonderoga, for the longer he stayed, the worse matters were bound to get. The nights were getting colder, and his troops had no winter clothing. Food was scarce, consisting mainly of salt pork and flour, and there was so little even of this that Burgoyne cut rations one third on October 3. All of the grass in the river meadows had been cropped, and horses began to starve and die. There was no grain, and Morgan's sharpshooters, by their continual raiding and sniping, kept foraging parties bottled up in camp. The reek of defeat and disaster was spreading through the entire army; the soldiers could sense and smell it even if Burgoyne could not—and as a result, desertions increased. Burgoyne tried to stop them by hanging deserters who were caught or, in some instances, sentencing them to an even more brutal and equally final punishment— 1000 lashes on their bare backs. Not even these extreme measures, however, could put an end to the desertions; the army continued slowly to waste away.

Gates, sitting smug and increasingly secure on Bemis Heights, was perfectly well aware of his adversary's problems. He had calculated on this all along. And knowing Burgoyne's reputation from the past, he anticipated with equal shrewdness exactly what Burgoyne's next move would be.

In a perceptive letter to New York Governor George Clinton, Gates wrote of Burgoyne: ". . . perhaps his despair may dictate to him to risk all upon one throw; he is an Old Gamester and in his time has seen many chances."

Gates was uncannily correct. The "Old Gamester" was now about to make his last roll of the dice.

CHAPTER FOURTEEN

The Showdown

GENTLEMAN JOHNNY BURGOYNE's battlefield tactics were self-defeating for two reasons: when he should have attacked, he didn't; when he shouldn't, he did. The opportunity that had beckoned to him on September 19 and 20 and 21 was no longer there. The high hill on the American left, which had been unprotected in those September days, was unprotected no longer. The Americans had fortified it; it was no longer there for easy taking. But Burgoyne did not know this. So thoroughly had Morgan's riflemen screened the woods and bottled him up in his own camp that he could not send out scouts to reconnoiter; he was without intelligence about American dispositions; he was fumbling in the dark like a blind man—he could not see his opponent nor did he know where he was.

In the interval between battles, Burgoyne had kept his army busy fortifying his line. It ran in a wide horseshoe from the river, up across the slope of Freeman's Farm toward the American lines; from there, it curved back to the north to the great ravine that ran behind the British position. The line was anchored by three principal fortifications. Near the river, the British had built what they called the "Great Redoubt," bristling with guns to cover the accumulated stores and ammunition and to

protect a pontoon bridge Burgoyne had built across the Hudson
to give his forces an avenue of retreat to the east if that
became necessary. The Balcarres Redoubt, named after the
earl, strengthened the center at Freeman's Farm; and at the
extreme end of the other prong of the horseshoe, the Breymann
Redoubt, also horseshoe-shaped, protected the extreme right at
the edge of the great ravine. Trees had been felled for 100 yards
in front of this line to give a clear field of fire. The weakest spot
was on the right wing between the Balcarres and Breymann
redoubts, a stretch of ground that was held by Canadian troops
protected only by two stockaded log cabins.

It was from these fortifications that the "Old Gamester" now
proposed to sally forth to risk all on one final gamble with fate.
On October 4, he called his top generals—Fraser, Riedesel and
Phillips—to a council of war.

Burgoyne had a battle plan already perfected in his mind, one
that was so foolhardy it seems to have shocked them all. He
proposed to leave only 800 men in the Great Redoubt to guard
his base camp and supplies; he planned to take the rest, some
4000 in all, and circle the enemy's left as Fraser had started to
do in the battle of September 19. Once he had gained position
on the Americans' left and rear, he would launch an all-out
attack with his whole force in an effort to drive them into the
river.

The generals took a dim view of the plan. Baron von Riedesel
later wrote that they doubted "whether 800 men would be
sufficient for the purpose assigned them. The safety of the whole
army depended upon this; for if this force should be beaten and
the bridges taken in its rear, then the entire army would be cut
off, and even if this detachment held its ground the position
might still be lost—since, as three or four days were necessary
to get through the woods and pathless thickets, the enemy would
have abundance of time to mass his force on this spot, when he
would, in all probability, capture the men and destroy the two
bridges—the only means of retreat."

Riedesel was thinking like a good general, but neither he nor
the others were capable of reading Gates's character as Gates

had read Burgoyne's. Given Gates's supercaution and his determination not to risk battle beyond his own lines, it is by no means certain that he would have challenged the British by assaulting their base camp with his right wing. He had not done this when the opportunity offered in the First Battle of Freeman's Farm, and his whole strategy was based upon making Burgoyne come to him and attack his lines. If he had sat and waited, as he might well have done, Burgoyne's wild gamble might have had a chance.

It was not to be. The council of war postponed decision for one day to study the surrounding landscape and try to assess the ability of a small rear guard to protect their river base. When the council met again, Riedesel voiced the opinion that it would be impossible to circle the American left in one day. He argued that the army should recross the Hudson and try to re-establish communications with Canada. Fraser agreed with him. Phillips refused to give an opinion.

All that this accomplished was the formulation of a compromise that had nothing to recommend it. Bulldog Johnny Burgoyne simply was not going to retreat. He decided to make the same essential movement against the American left, but now with a dangerously small force. According to Riedesel, Burgoyne decided that "on the 7th, he would undertake another great reconnoitering expedition against the enemy's left wing, to ascertain definitely his position, and whether it would be advisable to attack him. Should the latter be the case, he intended to advance on the enemy on the 8th with his entire army . . ."

On the morning of October 7—another of those clear, crisp autumn days with the sun shining on the multicolored foliage of the trees—Burgoyne gathered some 1600 of his best troops and set out to probe the American left. He sent some 600 rangers, Canadian auxiliaries, and the few Indians he had left to make a long circuit to the west, evidently hoping to draw the attention of the Americans in that direction. Then he led the main thrust from the entrenchments around Freeman's Farm. The advance was made by three closely knit columns carrying with them eight pieces of field artillery and two howitzers. General Frazer commanded the right with Balcarres' light infantry under him; Riedesel had the center; and the left was composed of a crack grenadier battalion from Fraser's corps under the command of Major John Acland.

The British advanced about 1000 yards toward the American lines until they came to a wheat field crowned by a slight ridge. Here the whole movement came to a halt. The troops fanned out in line and sat down on the edge of the wheat field. Why? Burgoyne had decided to call up his foragers to harvest the wheat!

No more ridiculous decision was ever made by a battlefield commander. This was not an attack; it was an invitation to disaster. Burgoyne's troops were spread out in a thin line 1000 yards long with only two men to hold every three yards. There they sat, waiting for the Americans to come and get them.

The British generals climbed to the roof of a log cabin behind the wheat field and strained their eyes trying to pick out features of the American line. But the autumn foliage hid everything; they could learn nothing of value. All that was being accomplished was a little foraging, hardly a task on which to risk 1600 men.

Gates first learned of the British movement when American pickets across Mill Creek fired some scattered shots. He sent James Wilkinson to investigate. Wilkinson galloped to the front, mounted a small rise, and for fifteen minutes watched the British antics. He spotted their generals on the roof of the log cabin and saw their foragers gathering in the wheat. Returning, he reported to Gates that the ground in front of the British was wide open, but their flanks rested on woods, ideal for Morgan's fighting riflemen. He told Gates that the British "offer you battle," and added, "I would indulge them."

"Well, then," said Gates, "order Morgan to begin the game."

Wilkinson makes no mention of a discussion that apparently followed this order. But Ebenezer Mattoon, a Continental officer who was at Gates's headquarters at the time, later reported to Philip Schuyler that there was quite an argument among Gates, Arnold, and Lincoln. Arnold, referring to Gates's order to commit just Morgan's riflemen and Dearborn's light infantry, argued:

"That is nothing; you must send a strong force."

Gates: "General Arnold, I have nothing for you to do; you have no business here."

Arnold's reply, Mattoon wrote, "was reproachful and severe."

Lincoln said: "You must send a strong force to support Morgan and Dearborn, at least three regiments."

Tugged and hauled in this fashion, Gates agreed to send Poor's brigade—composed of three regiments of New Hampshire Continentals, two New York regiments, and two regiments of Connecticut militia, probably about 800 in all—to attack the British left while Morgan attacked their right. Since Morgan had a longer and more circuitous march to make, Poor's men got into position first; and about two-thirty in the afternoon they opened what was to become known as the Second Battle of Freeman's Farm or, as it is sometimes called, the Battle of Bemis Heights.

Poor's target was the line of British grenadiers commanded by Major Acland. The grenadiers were stationed on a slight rise of ground above the wheat field, and Poor's brigade charged up the slope toward them. Acland's troops delivered a heavy volley of musket fire and a fusillade of grapeshot from their twelve-pounder cannon. It appears, however, that they did not allow sufficiently for the slope of the ground, most of their shots flying wildly over the heads of the charging Americans and riddling only the foliage and limbs of trees. Acland then ordered a bayonet charge, but Poor's men, who had held their fire, now loosed a deadly blast at point-blank range, riddling grenadiers who charged in line, shoulder to shoulder. Acland himself fell, shot through both legs.

The grenadiers delivered a second volley, this time with greater effect, taking a toll among the American ranks; but Poor's men, now wild with battle, surged forward yelling like madmen and swarmed over the grenadiers. They seized the twelve-pounder, swung it around, and began to use it against the British. Outnumbered three to one, the British left wing was crushed and fell back, small knots of grenadiers, virtually surrounded, still fighting stubbornly.

Now Morgan struck against the exposed right. He had scattered the advance screen of rangers, Canadians, and Indians that Burgoyne had sent out wide on this flank; he had advanced through the woods with his riflemen; and now he fell like a thunderbolt—or, in Wilkinson's words "like a torrent"—on the flank and rear of the British right wing. The British were posted behind a rail fence, and Balcarres tried to swing his line to meet the encircling movement; but as he did, Dearborn's light infantry charged with ferocity. Under attack both front and flank, Balcarres' troops broke and fell back to a second rail fence, where their commander tried to rally them. But the troops of Morgan and Dearborn, in a frenzy of battle fervor, stormed through this second line and drove Balcarres' troops from the field, capturing all of their cannon.

This left only the advanced center under Riedesel, whose stubborn German troops held their position. They were exposed on both flanks by the rout of the British left and right wings, but still they stood.

Now another American brigade, led by Ebenezer Learned, swept on the field; and with it appeared a stocky, powerful figure, clad in the uniform of an American general and mounted on a huge, furiously galloping brown horse. Benedict Arnold, throwing off all restraint, defying Gates, had come to battle.

Shunted aside, having no command and no role to play, Arnold had been beside himself as the sounds of battle welled. Mounted upon his great horse, he rode up and down the American encampment, venting his wrath. Finally, he could stand it no longer. Digging his spurs into his horse's sides, he shouted, "Victory or death!" and burst in a furious gallop from the American entrenchments, riding toward the heart of the battle.

Gates, possessed as always by the fear that this headlong fighter "might do some rash thing," ordered one of his aides, Major John Armstrong to catch Arnold and bring him back. But Arnold, seeing Armstrong coming and sensing his purpose, galloped all the harder. What ensued was sheer farce—the spectacle of the Americans' greatest field commander being pursued all over the battlefield by an officer intent on ordering him to stop fighting and come back.

The first troops Arnold caught up with were some of Poor's Connecticut militia.

"Whose regiment is that?" he shouted.

"Colonel Lattimer's, sir."

"Ah! My old Norwich and New London friends," Arnold cried. "God bless you! I'm glad to see you."

He spurred on and caught up with the head of Learned's brigade. The troops gave their old general a rousing cheer; and Arnold, waving his sword, shouting to his men, the demon of the battlefield, placed himself at the head of three of Learned's regiments and launched them in a charge across Mill Creek and up the slope directly at Riedesel's embattled Brunswickers. Strengthened at the last minute by two other German regiments, Riedesel's men poured out a deadly fire, and Learned's troops, unable to stand before it, broke and retreated down the slope.

With the Germans in the center fighting on three fronts, with the British line on either side broken into fragments, General Simon Fraser now tried to rally his troops around the British 24th Regiment and the light infantry. Fraser was the British counterpart of Arnold, the one inspiring leader who might have stemmed the tide of defeat. He charged up and down the line, shouting to his men, ordering them into position, and the broken regiments began to respond to his magnetic presence.

The British were already as good as beaten, but there is a vast difference between defeat and rout. Benedict Arnold would settle for nothing less than the rout; and charging up to Morgan, he pointed to Fraser and said: "That man on the gray horse is a host in himself and must be disposed of."

Morgan gathered his ace sharpshooters around him. The words he is quoted as having said do not sound like Dan Morgan, but then this was an age in which historians liked to dress up ruthless orders in fancy language. And so, as it has come down to us, this is the way Morgan relayed Arnold's order:

"That gallant officer is General Fraser. I admire and honor him, but it is necessary that he should die; victory for the enemy depends upon him. Take your station in that clump of bushes and do your duty."

The riflemen took cover in the bushes and began to fire at Simon Fraser. One bullet cut the crupper of his horse; the next passed through its mane. Aides urged Fraser to draw back, to expose himself no longer; but Fraser, like Arnold, defied the bullets that flew around him.

Timothy Murphy had not bothered with the bushes. Cradling his double-barreled rifle, he had climbed a medium-sized tree and settled himself in an upper crotch. There he drew a bead on General Fraser, nearly 300 yards away. At the crack of his rifle, Fraser fell, shot through the stomach, mortally wounded.

There would be some dispute almost two centuries later, another nit-picking quarrel among historians, about whether Timothy Murphy was really the one who fired this shot; but among the men of the Revolution at the time, there was no dissent. The later version would have it that some unnamed rifleman wearing a floppy hat crawled out of the bushes after shooting Fraser; but Fraser himself, before he died, said that he saw the man who shot him, perched high up in a tree—Tim Murphy's spot. The weight of the evidence certainly seems to be now, as it was at the time, that sharp-eyed Tim Murphy was the rifleman who fired what has been called the single most important shot of the Revolution. For, with the fall of Fraser, the heart went out of the British troops. The whole line gave way and fell back pell-mell into the shelter of the British fortifications.

Here the battle might have ended except for one man, Benedict Arnold. Brigadier General Abraham Ten Broeck with his brigade of 3000 New York militia—some of them veterans who had fought with Herkimer at Oriskany—had just arrived on the field. Arnold, charging wildly up and down, having no authority at all, simply seized command of every regiment in sight and hurled them headlong at the Balcarres Redoubt in the center of the British fortified line. Balcarres' cannon had a clear field of fire; and though the charging Americans penetrated the abatis at the bottom of the slope, the hail of grapeshot and musketry was too much for them. They fell back in disorder.

Major Armstrong was still pursuing Benedict Arnold—and still failing to catch him. Arnold was a whirlwind, in perpetual motion. Balked in his frontal attack on the Balcarres Redoubt, he spotted some of Learned's men getting into position off to his left, and he set off at a gallop directly across the whole field of fire from Balcarres' lines in order to reach them. Every gun in the British ranks seemed aimed at him; musket balls flew all around him. Watching in horror, the pursuing Major Armstrong decided prudently not to attempt to follow through that deadly barrage.

By some miracle unscathed, Arnold galloped up to the head of Learned's regiments and, either by instinct or good luck, led them in a charge against the weakest sector of the British line—that stretch of palisaded ground, held by unsteady Canadian troops, that ran between the Balcarres and Breymann redoubts. In one wild charge, Learned's troops, whipped on by Arnold, roared over the defenders and breached the main line of the British fortifications.

Still Arnold was not done. Raging everywhere, he gathered up Morgan's riflemen, two regiments of Continentals, and Colonel John Brooks's Massachusetts regiment that had just come on the field. Swerving to his left, he flung these forces at the Breymann Redoubt, the vital anchor of the British right wing. The redoubt was a stout breastwork made of logs laid between perpendicular posts. It was 200 yards long and sat on a knoll, its cannon commanding a clear sweep of ground to the southwest. Originally manned by 500 men, its garrison had been reduced to 200 by drafts on Breymann's forces to bolster other sectors of the line. This was a paper-thin force to withstand the impetuous charge of Arnold. Riding around the redoubt, waving his sword, shouting to his men to come on, he led a furious onslaught, leaping his great brown horse through a sally port. There the horse was shot under him, and Arnold's leg and thigh were crushed under the horse in the fall.

The shot that brought down Arnold was fired by a wounded German soldier lying on the ground. Brooks's soldiers, storming into the redoubt after Arnold, were about to dispatch the German who had felled their leader when Arnold stopped them, crying: "Don't hurt him, he's a fine fellow! He only did his duty."

The battle was over now. Breymann, trying to rally his men, flailing at them with his sword, was killed by one of his own troopers; in panic, the rest fled. The entire British line had been broken and turned; the Balcarres Redoubt could no longer be held. Burgoyne's forces were swept back to their last refuge, the Great Redoubt that guarded their base camp by the river.

Benedict Arnold, in his furious charges up and down and across the battlefield, had insured victory, total and complete; and as he lay there in the Breymann Redoubt, his crushed leg under him, the pursuing Major Armstrong finally caught up with him. History does not record what Major Armstrong said. It must have sounded ridiculous if, after this day of battle, he had delivered the intended injunction: "Sir, General Gates orders you to stay behind our lines."

It did not matter now. Benedict Arnold had led American troops in battle for the last time; for him, only treason lay ahead. Treason that would result from his own all-consuming vanity, his passion for high living beyond his means, his infatuation for a beautiful Tory, Peggy Shippen, who would agree to become his wife only, it seems, if he would join her cause.

All that lay in the future, unsuspected, unreadable, as the impassioned fighter who had stormed all over the field in this climactic battle was lifted on a litter and carried back to those lines on Bemis Heights that Gates had forbidden him to leave. Just before the blackness of unconsciousness descended upon him, Benedict Arnold, indomitable as ever, gave his final order of the day: he refused to let the surgeons cut off his shattered leg.

 *Surrender*

BURGOYNE and his army now were doomed. The Second Battle of Freeman's Farm had been an unparalleled disaster. Burgoyne had lost approximately half of the 1600 men with whom he had started out on the morning of October 7. Total casualty figures are uncertain; but the Americans had taken 240 prisoners, and when Burgoyne retreated from the Great Redoubt, he abandoned more than 300 sick and wounded. American casualties, both killed and wounded, were only about 150.

In the aftermath of the battle, the top commanders on both sides, Gates and Burgoyne, distinguished themselves by their incompetence. The shattering defeat had left Burgoyne with just one sensible choice: to retreat as swiftly as possible and try to get back to Canada before he was completely cut off and hemmed in. Gates, whose victorious army now occupied the former British lines across Freeman's Farm and above the great ravine, had a beaten enemy before him and a rare opportunity to fall upon that enemy in all the inevitable disarray of retreat. But for days both sat and did nothing.

One effect of the great American victory was, however, predictable: the countryside was swarming in unprecedented numbers. Aroused militia had been joining Gates ever since the

legend of the scalping of Jane McCrea had gained wide cur-
rency, but there is no tonic like that of a tremendous victory,
and American militia, eager now to be in at the kill, swarmed
from every hill and dale. Before many days had passed, the
American forces swarming around Burgoyne's hapless army
had swelled to more than 18,000 men.

All day October 8 Burgoyne made preparations for retreat.
He must have known from the beginning that it would be a
hazardous maneuver. Even before the battle of the seventh,
Gates had sent Brigadier General John Fellows with 1300
militia up the east side of the Hudson to the Battenkill. There
they had crossed the Hudson to Saratoga, positioning themselves in Burgoyne's rear. They were a slight, irregular force
that at the moment posed no serious threat, but, unless Burgoyne
moved swiftly, they could be joined and reinforced by others—
and then the threat would be serious indeed.

Swift movement, unfortunately for Burgoyne and unfortunately for his army, was a tactic that was foreign to the indolent
nature of Gentleman Johnny. He began his retreat at ten o'clock
of the dark night of October 8 after breaking up his pontoon
bridge across the Hudson. He loaded the boats that had been
used to form the bridge with supplies and sent them struggling
upstream against the current. He moved his army overland
along the west bank, led by Riedesel. To cloak the retreat,
camp watch fires were kept burning throughout the night, and
though the British "every moment expected to be attacked,"
they stole cleanly away without a single American lookout bay-
ing the alarm.

The weather now turned beastly. Rain came down in torrents.
The road, bad at best, became a quagmire of sucking mud.
Wagons stuck fast; the weary soldiers struggled to drag their
feet out of the clinging muck. Still Burgoyne persisted in hauling
along with him all his remaining cannon and a lot of unnecessary
baggage.

"At six o'clock in the morning," Baroness von Riedesel wrote,
"a halt was made, at which everyone wondered. General
Burgoyne had all the cannon ranged and counted, which wor-

ried us all, as a few more good marches would have placed us in security."

Burgoyne waited for his bateaux to catch up, and the army did not move again until four o'clock in the afternoon of October 9. Von Riedesel thought this delay was inexcusable, that a determined forced march—the kind St. Clair had made from Ticonderoga, for example—would have taken the army to Saratoga well ahead of any sizable American force that could have been gathered to cut it off. There a bridge could have been thrown quickly across the narrow stream, and the army could have been well on its way to Canada.

Instead of acting with this kind of speed and dispatch, Burgoyne, even after he broke camp late on the afternoon of October 9, crawled forward only a short distance—and stopped again. "Toward evening," Baroness von Riedesel wrote, "we at last came to Saratoga, which was only a half hour's march from the place where we had spent the whole day."

Fellows' weak militia force, which had positioned itself at Saratoga before Burgoyne arrived, could have been attacked and routed with ease; but Burgoyne, in no mood to fight, let them go and in the night they all escaped across the river. There they were soon joined by some 1100 more New Hampshire militia led by that skillful, contrary, unpredictable fighter John Stark, now coming on the field to cut off the escape route up the lakes to Canada.

Having reached Saratoga, Burgoyne sat down to enjoy himself, at least for one more evening. He established himself in Philip Schuyler's fine mansion, located above the river. As one German account later put it:

"While the army was suffering from cold and hunger, and everyone was looking forward to the immediate future with apprehension, Schuyler's house was illuminated, and rung with singing, laughter, and the jingling of glasses. There Burgoyne was sitting, with some merry companions, at a dainty supper, while the champagne was flowing. Near him sat the beautiful wife of an English commissary, his mistress . . . Some were of the opinion that he had made that inexcusable stand, merely for the sake of passing a merry night. Riedesel thought it incumbent on him to remind Burgoyne of the danger of the halt, but the latter returned all sorts of evasive answers."

And what was Horatio Gates doing all this time while opportunity beckoned? He was sitting on his haunches on Bemis Heights, doing virtually nothing.

Gates did not move forward until October 10; but then the Americans, traveling light, not encumbered with the kind of heavy baggage the British dragged along, moved so swiftly that by late afternoon they were in sight of Burgoyne's lines above Saratoga. Gates planned an attack for the early morning of October 11, but a heavy fog shrouded the field and fouled up the maneuver. When the fog lifted, the Americans saw how strong the British position was and retreated under fire. They then concentrated on Burgoyne's bateaux in the river and before the day was over had captured most of them.

This half-hearted stab at Burgoyne's lines had had just one other result. Burgoyne set fire to Schuyler's handsome mansion and its surrounding buildings. He claimed later that he had ordered the destruction because the buildings masked the field of fire from some of his artillery, but Riedesel, like the Americans, thought the burning of the mansion was unnecessary—the work of "wicked hands."

Even after this destruction of the mansion in which he had caroused so happily, Burgoyne sat on, like a man chained to the ground. The Americans had now fanned out around three sides of his position. Only his rear, that vital path to the north, remained open, and only the most unrealistic optimist could have imagined it would stay open for long. Riedesel urged that the army abandon all its baggage and march swiftly up the west side of the Hudson, crossing above Fort Edward. Burgoyne, stubborn to the end, would not agree.

While he dallied, the circle tightened. The Americans established three batteries of artillery across the narrow Hudson, and Morgan's riflemen infested the outskirts of the British camp. Baroness von Riedesel wrote that "a frightful cannonade began, principally directed against the house in which we had sought shelter, probably because the enemy believed, from seeing so many people flocking around it, that all the generals made it their headquarters. Alas! it harbored none but wounded soldiers or women!"

The baroness and her children sought refuge in the cellar of the house. The stench of rotting horses and oxen, dead from starvation or killed by cannon balls, was spreading in a smothering, gagging blanket over the camp.

The following morning the baroness had barely time to clean out the cellar "when a fresh and terrible cannonade threw us all once more into alarm . . . Eleven cannon balls went through the house, and we could plainly hear them rolling over our heads. One poor soldier, whose leg they were about to amputate, having been laid upon the table for this purpose, had the other leg taken off by another cannon ball in the very middle of the operation. His comrades all ran off, and when they came back, they found him in one corner of the room, where he rolled in his anguish, scarcely breathing . . ."

Burgoyne's army was in the direst straits. Each hour made the situation more desperate. Gentleman Johnny, who had bungled at every opportunity to bungle, now turned to that other bungler, Colonel Philip Skene, and said: "You have brought me to this pass. Now tell me how to get out of it."

Skene, the ever-optimistic Tory with his overweening contempt of all rebels, suggested cynically: "Scatter your baggage, stores and everything that can be spared, at proper distances, and the militiamen will be so busy plundering them that you and your troops will get clean off."

Even now, Philip Skene could not imagine that the rebels were animated by ideals loftier than cheap plunder.

On October 12 Burgoyne called another council of war. It discussed five propositions: to wait where they were, hoping against hope for help from New York; to attack the enemy; to retreat with all their artillery and baggage, forcing the river fords at Fort Edward; to retreat by night, leaving everything behind that could not be carried, crossing the river above Fort Edward or marching around Lake George; and finally, if Gates should make a false movement, to still try to force a passage down to Albany.

Most of these proposals, given the desperate situation of the army, were obviously impracticable. Riedesel insisted that their only chance lay in the adoption of the fourth alternative—a quiet swift retreat in the night, unencumbered by artillery or baggage, each soldier to carry with him provisions for six days. It was finally agreed that this should be done. Riedesel distributed the rations and at ten o'clock at night, October 12, he asked headquarters for marching orders. The answer came back: "The retreat is postponed; the reason why is not known." Even at this eleventh hour, Burgoyne balked like a stubborn mule at taking the one last, obvious course that lay open to him.

He never had another chance. During the night the Americans crossed from the Battenkill on the east side of the river and erected a new battery on the west bank. John Stark had taken over command of the swelling militia forces in Burgoyne's rear, and the escape route to the north, so briefly open, was now effectively closed.

"Numerous parties of American militia . . . swarmed around the little adverse army like birds of prey," wrote Sergeant Lamb of the British Army. "Roaring of cannon and whistling of bullets from their rifle pieces were heard constantly day and night."

Riedesel, in his account written later, described the hopelessness of their position in these words:

"Every hour the position of the army grew more critical, and the prospect of salvation grew less and less. There was no place of safety for the baggage; and the ground was covered with dead horses that had either been killed by the enemy's bullets or by exhaustion . . . Even for the wounded, no spot could be found which could afford them a safe shelter—not even, indeed, for so long a time as might suffice a surgeon to bind up their ghastly wounds. The whole camp was now a scene of constant fighting. The soldier could not lay down his arms day or night, except to exchange his gun for the spade when new entrenchments were thrown up. The sick and wounded would drag themselves along to a quiet corner of the woods and lie down on the damp ground. Nor even here were they longer safe, since every little while a ball would come crashing down among the trees."

It could not go on forever. On October 13 Burgoyne called another council of war. It decided on surrender.

There followed some bickering between Burgoyne and Gates over the terms. With all the cards in his hands, Gates now waffled. Just as Sir Henry Clinton had looked fearfully behind him worrying about a possible descent by Washington upon New York, so Gates now began to look over his shoulder, worrying about a possible descent by Clinton upon Albany. And so, incredibly, he ended up on October 15 snatching eagerly at every item of the terms Burgoyne proposed to him.

Here were Burgoyne's demands: The British were to march out of camp with all the honors of war and ground their arms by the riverside at the command of their own officers. The troops of the surrendering army were not even to be considered prisoners of war; they were to be granted passage back to England from the port of Boston in British transports "whenever General Howe shall so order." All this was to be granted on their promise of "not serving again in North America during the present contest." The Americans were to provide rations for the surrendering army during its march to Boston and quarters for the troops when they arrived there. The officers were to keep all their baggage and horses on Burgoyne's personal pledge that "no public stores are secreted therein." The Canadians in the surrendering army were to be allowed to return to Canada, the Americans supplying them on their march. These agreements were not to be entitled a "Capitulation"—but a "Convention." So sweeping were the provisions that Burgoyne himself was stunned and suspicious when Gates fell all over himself in his haste to accept them, making just one stipulation—that the British surrender right away, no later than two o'clock the following afternoon.

Guessing that Gates must be worrying about Clinton, Burgoyne was tempted to reject the whole Convention, hoping

even now that Clinton might be engineering some master stroke
to help him, unaware that Clinton had no such intention. Another council of war was held, but Burgoyne's officers took the
position that since Gates had agreed to all the terms Burgoyne
himself had proposed, Burgoyne was honor-bound to abide
by them. And so, on the afternoon of October 16, Burgoyne
and his staff in their "rich, royal uniforms" rode out of camp
and met Gates, clad only in "a plain, blue frock."

"The fortune of war, General Gates," Burgoyne said, "has
made me your prisoner."

"I shall ever be ready to testify that it has not been through
any fault of your Excellency," Gates responded. Then he invited Burgoyne and his staff to dinner.

The surrender took place on the morning of October 17. It
was a colorful spectacle. The troops paraded at ten o'clock and
then marched out, as British Lieutenant Digby wrote, "with
drums beating and the honours of war, but the drums seemed
to have lost their inspiring sound, and though we beat the
'Grenadier's March,' which not long before was so animating,
yet then it seemed by its last effort, as if almost ashamed
to be heard on such an occasion."

The troops stacked their arms in a meadow by the river, then
marched through the American camp, between two lines drawn
up in order. By Gates's command, the conquering Americans
were silent; not a word, not a taunt was uttered. One of the captured Brunswickers studied his conquerors and, in some amaze-
ment, wrote this description of their appearance:

"Not one of them was properly uniformed, but each man had
on the clothes in which he goes to the field, to church or to the
tavern. But they stood like soldiers, erect, with a military bearing
that was subject to little criticism . . . Not one fellow made a
motion as if to speak to his neighbor; furthermore, nature had
formed all the fellows who stood in rank and file, so slender, so
handsome, so sinewy, that it was a pleasure to look at them
and we were all surprised at the sight of such finely built
people. And their size! . . . The officers . . . wore very few
uniforms and those they did wear were of their own invention.

All colors of cloth . . . brown coats with sea-green facing, white linings and silver sword-knots; also gray coats with straw facings and yellow buttons were frequently seen . . . The brigadiers and generals have special uniforms and ribbons which they wear like bands of order over the vests . . ."

One of the captives who faced the future with a fear born of uncertainty was Baroness von Riedesel. She rode out of camp with her three small children, not knowing what to expect. She described what happened next:

"When I approached the tents, a noble-looking man came toward me, took the children out of the wagon, embraced and kissed them, and then with tears in his eyes helped me also to alight. 'You tremble,' said he to me; 'fear nothing.' 'No,' replied I, 'for you have been so kind, and have been so tender toward my children, that it has inspired me with courage.'"

The "noble-looking man" conducted the baroness to Gates's tent, where Gates was already entertaining Burgoyne and Phillips. After Burgoyne had spoken kindly to her, telling her that her ordeal was over now, the stranger who had escorted her came up to her and said: "It may be embarrassing to you to dine with all these gentlemen; come now with your children into my tent, where I will give you, it is true, a frugal meal, but one that will be accompanied by the best of wishes."

The baroness went with the kindly man. Only later did she learn that he was Philip Schuyler, whose mansion and out-buildings at Saratoga Burgoyne had burned, perhaps needlessly. Schuyler, who had labored so hard to send up from Albany the supplies that had helped to make Gates's victory possible, had come to camp despite threats from the unreasonable New Englanders that he would be shot if he showed his face. He ignored the threats; he refused to harbor resentment over the destruction of his mansion; he outdid himself in kindnesses to the Baroness von Riedesel and her children—and, later, to Burgoyne himself. Philip Schuyler remained a big man to the last.

CHAPTER SIXTEEN

Dawn of a New Day

IT HAD BEEN one of the most decisive battles in the history of the world, and its effects turned out to be earth-shaking.

The American cause, battered by disaster after disaster, seemingly poised on the brink of destruction after the loss of Philadelphia and Washington's defeats at Brandywine and Germantown, was suddenly revived and more alive than ever. The chancellories of Europe, dubious before, were at last convinced. A ragtag army of amateur soldiers had met and completely destroyed an invading force led by experienced generals and composed of seasoned veterans of European battlefields. Shock waves from that event rippled across the world.

It was not just the victory, but the stunning, cataclysmic finality of it. The Americans had taken prisoner two lieutenant generals, two major generals, three brigadiers, the staffs and aides of all of them, and 299 other officers of all ranks. The British and Germans had lost 1429 men killed and wounded, and, as it turned out, after the surrender 4836 privates became prisoners of war. All of the equipment in the hands of the invading army had been seized, and this was of enormous importance to rebelling colonists who had been so poorly supplied in all things. The war materiel taken with Burgoyne in the final surrender included 27 cannon of various calibers, 5000 stand of small arms, and large quantities of ammunition and military equipment of all kinds.

There was to be one ugly aftermath. The "Convention" of surrender, to which Gates had so hastily agreed, was to be repudiated by the Continental Congress on the grounds the British intended to violate it anyway. Gates clearly had acted in panic and folly to have accepted such a one-sided document, but he had pledged his word and, through him, the nation had pledged its word. But the Americans went back on the promises made to Burgoyne, and the British prisoners were marched off into the interior of Virginia, where they were held until war's end.

This mattered little at the time. What mattered were the strategic and diplomatic effects of the great, watershed victory at Saratoga. With Burgoyne's surrender, British troops gave up Crown Point and Ticonderoga and retreated into Canada. The threat from the North, the danger of a two-pronged drive that might split the colonies apart, was ended for the duration of the war. Nothing like Burgoyne's ambitious campaign would ever be tried again.

Of even greater importance was the diplomatic fallout of Saratoga. News of Burgoyne's surrender reached Paris on December 5, 1777. The British historian George Otto Trevelyan recorded the French reaction in these words: "When the news of Saratoga spread abroad in the city, the partisans of England disappeared from view; the theatres resounded with martial demonstrations; and the buzz of drawing-rooms and coffee-houses swelled into a unanimous cry for war."

The response of the French government was practically automatic. On December 6, King Louis XVI recognized the independence of the United States. This was just the first step. On February 6, 1778 France signed a formal Treaty of Alliance with America. The French were now in the war, an event of pivotal importance. It meant that the large French navy would contest the British for control of the seas and eventually make possible the final victory at Yorktown. It meant that thousands of trained French soldiers and vast quantities of war materiel of all kinds would now flow in an unending stream to the impoverished American armies. And it meant even more than this. With France in the war, Spain would soon follow. The conflict that had begun as a limited colonial rebellion swelled, as a result of Saratoga, into a world-wide collision, pitting the British against their ancient enemies, some of the strongest nations in Europe.

Saratoga, then, was the victory that made the final victory possible. Sir Edward Creasy was later to write in *The Fifteen Decisive Battles of the World:* "Nor can any military event be said to have exercised more important influence on the future fortunes of mankind, than the complete defeat of Burgoyne's expedition in 1777; a defeat which rescued the revolted colonists from certain subjection; and which, by inducing the courts of France and Spain to attack England in their behalf, ensured the independence of the United States, and the formation of the Transatlantic power which, not only America, but both Europe and Asia, now see and feel."

On that bright October morning when Burgoyne's troops marched out and stacked their guns in surrender on the field of Saratoga, it was the dawn of a new era—the dawn of a new nation and, indeed, of a whole new philosophy of democratic government by the people; an idea that would spread and gather force until, ultimately, it would rock all the thrones of Europe.

INDEX